Knitting
in No Time

Knitting in No Time

A Fast, Fun Collection of 50 Quick-Knit Projects

Melody Griffiths

Reader's
Digest

The Reader's Digest Association, Inc.
Pleasantville, New York/Montreal/Sydney

A READER'S DIGEST BOOK
This edition published by
The Reader's Digest Association, Inc.
by arrangement with Cico Books
32 Great Sutton Street
London EC1V 0NB

FOR CICO BOOKS
Photography: Tino Tedaldi
Editor: Eleanor van Zandt
Design: Alison Shackleton

FOR READER'S DIGEST

U.S. Project Editor: Marilyn J. Knowlton
Consulting Editor: Jane Townswick
Canadian Project Editor: Pamela Johnson
Associate Art Director: George McKeon
Executive Editor, Trade Publishing: Dolores York
President & Publisher, Trade Books: Harold Clarke

Cover photograph: Christine Bronico

Library of Congress Cataloging-in-Publication Data

Griffiths, Melody.
    Knitting in No Time : a fast, fun collection of quick-knit project / Melody Griffiths.
        p. cm.
    ISBN 0-7621-0665-4
    1. Knitting—Patterns. I. Title

TT825.G684 2005
746.43'2–dc22

2005044734

Address any comments about
Knitting in No Time to:
The Reader's Digest Association, Inc.
Adult Trade Publishing
Reader's Digest Road
Pleasantville, NY 10570-7000

For more Reader's Digest products and information, visit our website:
www.rd.com (in the United States)
www.rd.ca (in Canada)
www.readersdigest.com.au (in Australia)
Printed in China
1 3 5 7 9 10 8 6 4 2

CONTENTS

Introduction   6

SCARVES, HATS, AND GLOVES 8

Lacy scarf   10
Diagonal scarf   12
Beaded-rib scarf   14
Scrap-yarn scarf   16
Wavy scarf   18
Quick-to-knit earflap hat   20
Pull-on hat and hand warmers   22
Skinny scarf   26
Fair Isle earflap hat   28
Fair Isle fingerless gloves   32
Floppy-brim hat   34
Rainbow scarf   36
Braided scarf   38
Pom-pom scarf   40
Scattered-sequin scarf   42
Leg warmers   44
Leopard-spotted headband   46

WRAPS, PONCHOS, AND SHRUGS 48

Tassel wrap   50
Cream ribbed cowl   52
Fizz wrap   54
Comfort wrap   56
Ribbon-yarn wrap   58
Striped afghan   60
Fluffy shrug   62
Slouchy shrug   66
Summer shawl   68
Chevron poncho   70

JACKETS AND TOPS 72

Loop-edge jacket   74
Ripped-fabric top   78
Fun-fur vest   82
Wrap jacket   86
Sparkle vest   90
Sheepskin-look vest   92
Dip-and-rip vest   96
Shaded jacket   100
Circular sweater   104
Blanket jacket   108

BAGS 112

Denim bag   114
Chunky-knit tote   116
Weekend bag   118
Gold sequin bag   122
Moss-stitch bag   124
String bag   126
Knitting bag   128
Woven-look bag   130
Beaded cell-phone pouch   134
Tweed handbag   136
Black velvet bag   138
Scrap mini-bag   140

TECHNIQUES 142

The Basics   142
    Holding the yarn and needles   142
    Making a slip knot   143
    Casting on   144
    Binding off   145
    Making a knit stitch   146
    Making a purl stitch   147
Simple stitch patterns   148
    Garter stitch   148
    Rib   148
    Seed Stitch   148
    Stockinette stitch   148
How to cable   149
Shaping and patterning   150
    Increasing   150
    Decreasing   151
Making garments   152
    Understanding the instructions   152
    Finishing   153
Sewing up   154
    Grafting stitches   154
Making a twisted cord   155
Picking up a dropped stitch   155
Ten tips for faster knitting   156

Resources   157
Index   159
Acknowledgements   160

Introduction

I've been totally fascinated by knitting ever since I was a teenager. The thing I love most is when that magic combination of tradition and innovation happens, and the technique, shape, yarn, and stitch pattern lock together to create something unique. As a designer, I'm meticulous about the decisions I need to make to get the shape and style I want, but when I start to knit, the rhythm takes over and time disappears.

This collection of 50 designs shows you how to create stylish, unusual accessories, and stunning garments using the simplest and quickest of stitches and techniques. There are designs for complete beginners, there are designs worked in the round, and there are designs for more adventurous or experienced knitters. The skills needed range from making a garter-stitch square mini-bag or working simple lengths of knitting for sumptuous scarves and wraps through to subtly shaped, fully fashioned jackets. But each design is planned to be as easy as possible for the techniques involved. Edgings are knitted in, row-by-row instructions are given wherever there is shaping, and there are hints and tips to help you get the best out of each design.

One of the joys of knitting is handling the yarn. There's such a huge choice available on the market now, so for the knits in this book, I've experimented with a range of wool and other natural fibers. Enjoy choosing from a variety of weights, or using scraps of left-over yarn mixed and matched for very different effects, or knitting up a soft, super-chunky yarn at speed. The patterns show you how to create simple knits in richly textured fashion yarns, and even how to improvise yarn with designs knitted in string or from ripped fabric strips.

With so many ideas to choose from, I hope that there is something right for you and that you are inspired to take pleasure in knitting for yourself, your family, and your friends. As a guide, each project has the time it took to make. Depending on your experience and enthusiasm, you may take more or less time than given. But however long it takes, remember that knitting isn't a speed competition—relaxation, enjoyment, and confidence in your creativity are far more important.

Melody

Scarves, hats, and gloves

Start with something simple like a scarf; then try knitting in the round to make hand and leg warmers or progress to shaping with fast, funky hats. A scarf is not only the traditional learn-to-knit project but also a vital fashion accessory. This section has 16 designs for you to choose from, including skinny scarves, scrap-yarn scarves, patterned scarves, and scarves with trims. Going around in circles creates tubes of knitting that can be used as hand, arm, or leg warmers. They're in a multicolored yarn that gives you instant stripes with no extra work. Super-chunky yarn and big needles make the simple earflap hat one of the fastest projects in this book.

- Lacy scarf
- Diagonal scarf
- Beaded-rib scarf
- Scrap-yarn scarf
- Wavy scarf
- Quick-to-knit earflap hat
- Pull-on hat and hand warmers
- Skinny scarf
- Fair Isle earflap hat and fingerless gloves
- Floppy-brim hat
- Rainbow scarf
- Braided scarf
- Pom-pom scarf
- Scattered-sequin scarf
- Leg warmers
- Leopard-spotted headband

Lacy scarf

The center of the scarf is knitted first; then the pointed edging is worked separately and sewn on. The lacy stitch for the center of the scarf is really very easy. The little motifs are placed at regular intervals. Every wrong-side row is just purl, and the stitch count remains the same throughout, so your fingers quickly learn what to do. Every wrong-side row of the edging is a knit row. The stitch count for the edging varies, but it's not hard to keep track of where you are in the pattern, and a stitch check is given each time the number of stitches changes.

ESTIMATED TIME TO COMPLETE
The scarf took 15 hours to knit.

ABOUT THIS YARN
Rowan Kid Silk Haze is 70% super kid mohair and 30% silk. It's incredibly soft and fine, with an approximate length of 229 yds. (210 m) to a 25 g (approx. 1 oz.) ball.

SIZE
Width inc. edging: 11 in. (28 cm); **length** inc. edging: 52 in. (132 cm).

YOU WILL NEED
• 2 x 25 g balls (approx. 2 oz.) of Rowan Kid Silk Haze in Jelly, shade 597
• pair of size US 8 (5 mm) knitting needles

GAUGE
20 sts and 22 rows to 4 in. (10 cm) over lace patt; edging measures 2⅜ in. (6 cm) at widest—both worked on US 8 (5 mm) needles and when pressed. Change needle size, if necessary, to obtain this gauge.

ABBREVIATIONS
k = knit; **patt** = pattern; **p** = purl; **RS** = right side; **skpo** = slip 1, k1, pass slipped st over; **sl** = slip 1 knitwise; **st(s)** = stitch(es); **tog** = together; **WS** = wrong side; **yo** = yarn forward and over needle to make a st; **[ ]** = work instructions in square brackets as directed.

NOTES
• Cast on loosely for the center of the scarf and for the edging.
• Bind off loosely when working the pointed edging. The bound-off edge of each point should be the same length as the increased edge.
• The needle size recommended is quite large for yarn this fine, which enhances the lacy effect and helps speed up the work. Although light, the yarn is amazingly strong, but you should handle it gently so the stitches slip easily along the needles; if they stick, your knitting is probably too tight—check your gauge again.

SCARF CENTER
Cast on 32 sts.
Row 1 (RS) K.
Row 2 (and every WS row) P.
Row 3 K3, [yo, skpo, k6] 3 times, yo, skpo, k3.
Row 5 K1, [k2tog, yo, k1, yo, skpo, k3] 3 times, k2tog, yo, k1, yo, skpo, k2.
Row 7 As Row 3.
Row 9 K.
Row 11 K7, [yo, skpo, k6] 3 times, k1.
Row 13 K5, [k2tog, yo, k1, yo, skpo, k3] 3 times, k3.
Row 15 As Row 11.
Row 16 P.
These 16 rows form the lace patt. Work 15 more repeats, then work 9 more rows. Bind off knitwise.

EDGING
Cast on 5 sts.
Row 1 (and every WS row) K.
Row 2 Sl 1, yo, k2tog, yo, k2. 6 sts.
Row 4 Sl 1, [yo, k2tog] twice, yo, k1. 7 sts.
Row 6 Sl 1, [yo, k2tog] twice, yo, k2. 8 sts.

Row 8 Sl 1, [yo, k2tog] 3 times, yo, k1. 9 sts.

Row 10 Sl 1, [yo, k2tog] 3 times, yo, k2. 10 sts.

Row 12 Sl 1, [yo, k2tog] 4 times, yo, k1. 11 sts.

Row 14 Sl 1, [yo, k2tog] 4 times, yo, k2. 12 sts.

Row 16 Bind off 8 sts loosely knitwise, 1 st on right needle, yo, k2tog, yo, k1. 5 sts.

These 16 rows form the edging patt. Work until edging fits around all four edges of the center of the scarf, allowing for easing around corners and ending with a complete repeat. Bind off.

TO FINISH

Join ends of edging. Placing seam in the middle of one long edge of the center of the scarf and overlapping edging, slip stich in place. Press the scarf according to yarn label, using a cloth to protect the knitting.

TIPS

● Instead of working a separate gauge swatch, you could just cast on the 32 sts for the center of the scarf and get started. The scarf, when pressed, should measure approximately 6¼ in. (16 cm) across.

● For a really neat join in the edging, cast on with a smooth, contrasting yarn. When the edging is long enough, don't bind off. Just undo the contrasting cast-on stitches, slipping loops onto a spare needle, then graft the ends together.

● When you join the ends of the edging, make sure first that it isn't twisted (see page 154).

Get the vintage effect with this pretty lacy scarf.

Diagonal scarf

The joy of working with this random-dyed yarn is that you get the effect of crazy stripes without having to change colors and deal with a lot of ends. An increase at the beginning and a decrease at the end on every right-side row make the stockinette stitch slant, emphasizing the stripes by tipping them at an angle.

ESTIMATED TIME TO COMPLETE
The scarf took 8 hours to knit.

ABOUT THIS YARN
Regia Multi Color 6-ply is a 75% wool, 25% polyamide yarn that's dyed to give a random-stripe effect when knitted. With approximately 137 yds. (125 m) to a 50 g (approx. 1¾ oz.) ball, the yarn goes a long way.

SIZE
Width: 4 in. (10 cm); **length:** approx. 67 in. (170 cm).

YOU WILL NEED
• 2 x 50 g balls (approx. 3½ oz.) of Regia Multi-Color 6-ply in Bonbon, shade 05404
• pair of size US 5 (3¾ mm) knitting needles

GAUGE
22 sts and 30 rows to 4 in. (10 cm) over st-st measured along the stitches and rows in the usual way; 19 sts measure 2¾ in. (7 cm) across st-st on the diagonal, all on size 5 (3¾ mm) needles. Change needle size, if necessary, to obtain this gauge.

ABBREVIATIONS
cont = continue; **k** = knit; **m1** = lift strand with left needle between sts and k into back of it; **p** = purl; **RS** = right side; **skpo** = slip 1, k1, pass slipped st over; **st(s)** = stitch(es); **st-st** = stockinette st; **WS** = wrong side.

NOTE
• Join in the second ball of yarn on the inner edge of the k4 edge sts.

TIPS

● Don't tie a big knot when joining in the new yarn. Just leave about 4 in. (10 cm) of the new yarn, cross the ends over each other, and carry on knitting. If the end left from the first ball is quite long, fold it over a couple of times and tie it in a slip knot to keep it out of the way.

● To weave in the yarn ends neatly, thread a tapestry needle with one end, check that the ends cross over, then—working vertically up the row ends and following the structure of the stitches—weave the end in around six or eight stitches. Stretch the knitting slightly to make sure the stitching doesn't pull the work in and that the end is secure, then cut off any excess yarn. Do the same with the other end, but taking it down the row ends.

TO KNIT
Cast on 27 sts. K 2 rows.
Work in diagonal st-st.
Row 1 (RS) K4, m1 k17, skpo, k4.
Row 2 K4, p19, k4.
These 2 rows form diagonal st-st.
Cont in diagonal st-st, work until scarf measures 67 in. (170 cm), ending with a RS row.
K 2 rows. Bind off knitwise.

TO FINISH
Weave in ends. Press according to yarn label.

This brightly-colored striped scarf can be wrapped, tied like a necktie, knotted, or even worn as a belt.

Beaded-rib scarf

This kind of beaded knitting is easy to do. You just knit in the usual way, bringing a bead up close to the work where indicated in the instructions. The beads hang between two purl stitches and show through on both sides of the scarf.

Jewel-bright silk-blend yarn and matte golden beads combine to make a scarf that will add instant glamour to any outfit.

SCARF

Start with a ball of yarn with approximately 200 beads threaded onto it.
Beaded cast-on. Leaving a long end, make a slip knot on the single, smaller needle. Using the knitting-off-the-thumb method on page 144, [B1, cast on 1 st] 33 times. 34 sts. Change to larger needles.
Row 1 (RS) K4, [p1, B1, p1, k2] to last 2 sts, k2.
Row 2 K2, [p2, k2] to end.
These 2 rows form a beaded rib with k2 at each end for edging.
Work in beaded rib for 138 more rows.
Using yarn without beads, cont for another 151 rows.
Change to beaded yarn and work 140 rows in beaded rib.
Bind off loosely in rib, bringing a bead up close between stitches each time.

TO FINISH

Weave in yarn ends. Using a cloth to protect the beads, press according to yarn label.

ESTIMATED TIME TO COMPLETE

The beads took an hour to thread, and the scarf took 21 hours to knit: 22 hours total.

ABOUT THIS YARN

Debbie Bliss Cathay is a mix of 50% cotton, 35% viscose microfiber, and 15% silk and is available in 12 jewel-bright shades. There are approx. 109 yds. (100 m) to a 50 g (approx. 1¾ oz.) ball.

SIZE

Width: beaded ends 4¼ in. (11 cm); center 4 in. (10 cm);
length: 67 in. (170 cm)

YOU WILL NEED

- 3 x 50 g balls (approx. 5¼ oz.) of Debbie Bliss Cathay in shade 03
- 1,046 beads (approx. 3½ oz. [100 g])
- one size US 3 (3¼ mm) knitting needle and a pair of size US 5 (3¾ mm) needles

GAUGE

30 sts and 26 rows to 4 in. (10 cm) over beaded rib, 34 sts and 24 rows to 4 in. (10 cm) over plain rib, both on size US 5 (3¾ mm) needles, when pressed. Change needle size, if necessary, to obtain these gauges.

ABBREVIATIONS

B1 = slide a bead up close to work; **cont** = continue; **k** = knit; **p** = purl; **RS** = right side; **st(s)** = stitch(es); **[ ]** = work instructions in square brackets as directed.

NOTES

- Thread half of the beads onto one ball of yarn before starting to knit. Thread the other half onto another ball.
- To thread beads onto the yarn, first tip beads into a shallow dish. Thread a sewing needle with a short length of sewing thread, and knot ends to make a loop. Slide the knot to one side and thread yarn end through loop. Pick up beads, 3 or 4 at a time, and slide them down the loop of thread and onto the yarn.
- Wash your beaded scarf by hand. Do not dry-clean. If you want to spin the scarf in the machine to remove excess water before drying, put it in a laundry bag or pillowcase to protect the beads from abrasion.

TIPS

● It's easier to hide the darned-in ends if you join a new ball of yarn inside the k2 edging.

● Sliding the beads along the yarn as you knit does take time. You may find it quicker to thread fewer beads onto the yarn—maybe around 200 at a time—then cut the yarn, add more beads, and join in again.

● Cathay would make a lovely scarf without the beads. You'll still need 3 x 50 g (approx. 5¼ oz.) balls of yarn. Simply work in rib with k2 edgings as given for 431 rows and bind off. Your scarf will be about 71 in. (180 cm) long.

● For the beaded edging you must cast on by the knitting-off-the-thumb method. Any other type of cast-on will hide the beads.

● You can use any type of bead, either matching or contrasting with the color you choose for your scarf. Just make sure that the beads have a center hole that's large enough to thread onto the yarn.

Design your own yarn mixture to create a sumptuously textured garter-stitch scarf.

Scrap-yarn scarf

Have some fun: Get out all those spare balls of yarn, pile them up, and sort them out. The idea is to combine between three and six strands of yarn to make a super-thick yarn that'll knit up quickly on big needles. If you don't have enough of a particular shade or texture, swap yarns with a friend or buy a ball or two of anything you fancy. The scarf pictured uses cream and other neutral shades with pale and bright pinks, and the yarns range from smooth and silky DK and Aran to textured mohair and chenille.

ESTIMATED TIME TO COMPLETE
There are only 20 stitches to a row, so if you can do a row in a minute and a half, the total knitting time will be around 4 hours. This does not allow for the time you spend deciding on which yarns and colors to put together.

SIZE
Width: 10 in. (25 cm); **length:** 53 in. (135 cm) not including tassels.

YOU WILL NEED
* approximately 18 oz. (500 g) of assorted yarns, such as brushed chunky, wool and wool mix, knitting worsted or DK, chenille, mohair, bouclé, and other textured yarns
* pair of size US 17 (12 mm) knitting needles

GAUGE
8 sts and 12 rows to 4 in. (10 cm) over gst using yarns stranded together on US size 17 (12 mm) needles. Change the number of yarns stranded together or the needle size, if necessary, to obtain this gauge.

ABBREVIATIONS
gst = garter stitch; **k** = knit; **st(s)** = stitch(es).

NOTE
* Strand 3 or more different-textured yarns together, changing the yarns and colors at random.

SCARF
Cast on 20 sts. Work in gst (every row k) changing colors and textures as desired until scarf measures approx. 53 in. (135 cm). Bind off.

TO FINISH
Weave in ends, if necessary (see Tips).

Fringe. You need 7 tassels for each end. For each tassel, cut 8-in. (20-cm) lengths, varying the number of strands according to the yarn thickness so that the tassels are all the same size. Fold the strands in half, slip the loop through the cast-on/bound-off edge, and pull the strands through. Trim ends evenly.

TIPS

● You can use almost any mixture of yarns for your scarf, but unless you know they are all machine-washable, it's best to hand-wash your scarf.

● If you change one strand of your mix at a time, anywhere along a row, you can knit the ends in as you go; this is stronger, neater, and faster than cutting all the yarns and joining at the beginning of a row.

● If you like, you could add more texture by joining in new yarns with a firm knot, then trimming the ends to 1–1½ in. (3–4cm) and leaving them to stick out decoratively.

● Of course, you could make the scarf longer or shorter, depending on the amount of yarn you have.

● If you'd like a wider or narrower scarf, cast on 4 stitches more or fewer for each 2-in. (5-cm) difference.

Wavy scarf

This easy-to-knit traditional Shetland stitch pattern is given a modern look by being worked in really thick, stranded cotton-mix yarn. There are only four rows to the pattern, and two of those are just knit! And on the lace row, each of the stitches made with a yarnover has a corresponding decrease, so the stitch count remains the same.

ESTIMATED TIME TO COMPLETE
The scarf took 19 hours to knit.

ABOUT THIS YARN
Spree is a lightweight but chunky, 60% cotton, 40% acrylic yarn with 150 yds. (137 m) to a 100 g (approx. 3½ oz.) ball. It's available in random-dyed colors, as well as naturals and blues.

SIZE
Width: 12¼ in. (31 cm); **length:** 75 in. (190 cm).

YOU WILL NEED
- 3 x 100 g balls (approx. 10½ oz.) of Sirdar Spree in White, shade 050 (A)
- 3 x 100 g balls (approx. 10½ oz.) of same in Faded Denim, shade 089 (B)
- pair of size US 10 (6 mm) knitting needles

GAUGE
20 sts and 20 rows to 4 in. (10 cm) over Old Shale patt on size US 10 (6 mm) needles. Change needle size, if necessary, to obtain this gauge.

ABBREVIATIONS
beg = beginning; **cont** = continue; **k** = knit; **patt** = pattern; **p** = purl; **RS** = right side; **skpo** = slip 1, k1, pass slipped st over; **st(s)** = stitch(es); **tog** = together; **yo** = take yarn over needle to make a st; **[ ]** = work instructions in square brackets as directed.

NOTE
- To avoid having lots of ends to darn in, see TIPS for how to change colors 3 stitches in from edge.

SCARF
Using A, cast on 61 sts.
Rows 1, 2, and 3 K.
Row 4 K3, p to last 3 sts, k3.
Row 5 (RS) K4, * [yo, k1] twice, yo, [skpo] 3 times, k1, [k2tog] 3 times, [yo, k1] 3 times, rep from * two more times, k3.
Row 6 K.
Rows 3–6 form the Old Shale patt. Cont in patt, work 4 rows B, 4 rows A until scarf measures 75 in. (190 cm), ending with **Row 6** in A. Cont in A, k 1 row. Bind off knitwise.

TIPS

- If your row gauge is correct, you'll have 95 wavy stripes, but in a scarf as big as this, it won't matter if you have a few stripes more or fewer, as long as you end with A to match the first stripe.

- When changing yarn colors, you'll get neater edges (and avoid having to darn in dozens of yarn ends) if you change color away from the edge and carry the unused color up the work until needed again. On the first color-change row, knit the 3 edge sts using B, weaving in the color A yarn, then continue using B only. On the following color-change rows, carry the yarn loosely across the 3 edge sts, then knit in the strand with the new color.

- To make a yarnover between two knit stitches, bring the yarn between the needles to the front of the work, then take it over the needle to knit the next stitch.

- If you want to make the scarf all in one color, you'll need only 5 x 100 g (approx. 10½ oz.) balls of Spree.

This generous scarf is a
gentle take on a nautical
theme.

TIPS

● Instead of knitting a gauge swatch, check your gauge by knitting an earflap. Cast on 7 sts with a smooth contrasting yarn, then change to Biggy Print and knit the earflap as directed. If the 5 sts in st-st measure 2¾ in. (7 cm) and your earflap is 3¼ in. (8 cm) long (excluding cast-on sts), then you can get on with the hat. Make a second earflap. Undo cast-on sts and sew earflaps onto finished hat.

● You'll find it easier to work the braids if you pin the earflap to the ironing board so the hat is held securely while you make the braid.

Quick-to-knit earflap hat

Incredibly thick, textured yarn and big needles make this a hat that you can conjure up in next to no time. Choose colors that match your favorite jacket or pick a bright contrasting shade for a modern look.

ESTIMATED TIME TO COMPLETE
The hat took 2 hours to knit.

SIZE
Around head: 21¼ in. (54 cm). This hat will fit an average woman's head.

YOU WILL NEED
- 2 x 100 g balls (approx. 7 oz.) of Rowan Biggy Print in Thunder, shade 252
- pair of size US 17 (12 mm) knitting needles

GAUGE
7 sts and 10 rows to 4 in. (10 cm) over st-st on size US 17 (12 mm) needles. Change needle size, if necessary, to obtain this gauge.

ABBREVIATIONS
k = knit; **kfb** = k into front and back of st; **RS** = right side; **skpo** = slip 1, k1, pass slipped st over; **s2kpo** = slip next 2 sts as if to k2tog, k1, pass 2 slipped sts over; **st(s)** = stitch(es); **st-st** = stockinette st; **tog** = together; **WS** = wrong side; **[ ]** = work instructions in square brackets as directed.

NOTE
- The gauge is firmer than usual for Biggy Print in stockinette stitch to give the hat a more sculptural shape.

TO FINISH
Join Rows 1 and 2, then wrap yarn around the knitting to make a top knot before joining remaining back seam. Cut 6 x 33½-in. (85-cm) lengths of yarn, and use 3 lengths threaded through fastened-off stitch at end of earflap and doubled, to make a 3-strand braid at the end of each earflap. Secure ends of braids with a length of yarn.

ABOUT THIS YARN
Biggy Print has two loosely twisted strands of varying thickness plied together to make a soft, but chunky 100% merino wool yarn that has 33 yds. (30 m) to a 100 g (approx. 3½ oz.) ball. This colorway has two tones of gray for the background with streaks of hot pink.

EARFLAP HAT
Cast on 5 sts.
Row 1 (RS) K.
Row 2 (and every WS row) P.
Row 3 [Kfb] 4 times, k1. 9 sts.
Row 5 [Kfb] 8 times, k1. 17 sts.
Row 7 [Kfb] 16 times, k1. 33 sts.
Row 9 K3, [kfb, k3] 7 times, k2. 40 sts. St-st 12 rows. Bind off knitwise.
Right earflap. With RS facing, leave first 6 sts of bound-off edge, working into back loop only, pick up one st from each of next 7 sts, turn.
Row 1 (WS) K1, p5, k1.

Row 2 K7.
Row 3 As Row 1.
Row 4 K1, k2tog, k1, skpo, k1. 5 sts.
Row 5 k1, p3, k1.
Row 6 K1, s2kpo, k1. 3 sts.
Row 7 k1, p1, k1.
Row 8 S2kpo. Fasten off.
Left earflap. With RS facing, leave center 14 sts of bound-off edge, working into back loop only, pick up 1 st from each of next 7 sts, turn.
Complete as given for right earflap.

Pull-on hat and hand warmers

This hat is a fine example of how easy and quick knitting can be. Simply work in rounds, using the knit stitch only, which produces stockinette stitch; the finishing is minimal. From casting on to wearing the hat took less than three hours.

If you have ever yearned for a Fair Isle or jazz-knitting effect, but just can't cope with more than one yarn at a time, the hand warmers shown at right are just perfect. The yarn itself creates the pattern, and although it is quite fine to work, it slips along the needles quickly. Watching the colors change is so fascinating that before you know it, you're halfway there.

The subtle colors in this hat allow you to coordinate it with many other projects in this book.

TIPS

● Every round of the hat shaping is given, so if you wish, you can check them off as you do them. If you look at the shaping rounds, you'll see that the number of stitches between increases is the same as the number of the round, so if you put the work down while increasing, you'll know where you are when you start again.

● Our instructions assume that you are working with a set of four double-pointed needles, starting with 2 sts and ending with 32 sts on each of 3 needles. If you have a set of 5 double-pointed needles, start off on 3 needles, as directed, and use the fourth needle to knit with. Then introduce the fifth needle on the 3rd round by working k3, kfb on the first needle and again on the second needle. You will end with 2 needles, each having 16 sts, while the other two have 32 sts.

◄ PULL-ON HAT AND SKINNY SCARF See instructions on pages 26–27 to make the skinny scarf.

ESTIMATED TIME TO COMPLETE
The hat took 3 hours to knit.

SIZE
Around brim: 20¾ in. (53 cm)

YOU WILL NEED
• 1 x 50 g ball (approx 1¾ oz.) of Noro Silk Garden in shade 89
• set of size US 8 (5 mm) double-pointed needles

GAUGE
18 sts and 24 rows to 4 in. (10 cm) over st-st on size US 8 (5 mm) needles. Change needle size, if necessary, to obtain this gauge.

ABBREVIATIONS
beg = beginning; **k** = knit; **kfb** = knit into front and back of st; **st(s)** = stitch(es); **st-st** = stockinette st; **[ ]** = work instructions in square brackets as directed.

ABOUT THIS YARN
This blend of 45% silk, 45% kid mohair, and 10% lamb's wool makes a soft, but springy fabric. It has approximately 109 yds. (100 m) to a 50 g (approx. 1¾ oz.) ball. The shaded colors create subtle stripes when knitted in the round.

TO KNIT
Cast on 6 sts. Using 2 needles and beg with a k row, st-st 6 rows. [Kfb] twice onto each of 3 needles. Join in a round. 12sts.
Round 1 [K1, kfb] 6 times. 18 sts.
Round 2 [K2, kfb] 6 times. 24 sts.
Round 3 [K3, kfb] 6 times. 30 sts.
Round 4 [K4, kfb] 6 times. 36 sts.
Round 5 [K5, kfb] 6 times. 42 sts.
Round 6 [K6, kfb] 6 times. 48 sts.
Round 7 [K7, kfb] 6 times. 54 sts.
Round 8 [K8, kfb] 6 times. 60 sts.
Round 9 [K9, kfb] 6 times. 66 sts.
Round 10 [K10, kfb] 6 times. 72 sts.
Round 11 [K11, kfb] 6 times. 78 sts.
Round 12 [K12, kfb] 6 times. 84 sts.
Round 13 [K13, kfb] 6 times. 90 sts.
Round 14 [K14, kfb] 6 times. 96 sts.
K every round for st-st until hat measures 8¾ in. (22.5 cm). Bind off.

TO FINISH
Join 6 rows at beg to make a stem, as shown top left. Weave in ends. Allow brim to roll.

TIPS

● If you have a set of 5 double-pointed needles, cast on 15 sts on each of 4 needles, join in a round, and complete the hand warmer as instructed.

● Knit a few rounds while traveling or waiting in line, and you'll soon be finished.

LEFT HAND WARMER

Cast on 20 sts on each of 3 needles. 60 sts. Taking care not to twist sts on needles, join in a round and k every round in st-st until hand warmer measures 7 in. (18 cm).
Thumb-opening round K50; leaving a long end, cut yarn. Using a length of smooth contrasting yarn, k7, rejoin Regia, k3. K every round until warmer measures 9½ in. (24.5 cm). Bind off.
Thumb. Undo contrasting sts, slip the 7 sts onto a needle and the 6 loops from row above onto another needle.
Round 1 Using first needle, k7, using 2nd needle, pick up 2 sts from row ends, k3 loops, using 3rd needle, k remaining 3 loops, pick up 2 sts from row ends. 17 sts. K 12 rounds. Bind off loosely.

RIGHT HAND WARMER

Work, as given, for left hand warmer to thumb-opening round.
Thumb-opening round K3, leaving a long end, cut yarn, using a length of smooth contrasting yarn, k7, rejoin Regia, k 50. Complete, as given, for left hand warmer.

TO FINISH

Weave in ends. Press according to yarn label.

ESTIMATED TIME TO COMPLETE
Each hand warmer takes about 2 hours to knit: 4 hours total.

SIZE
Circumference: 8 in. (20 cm); **length**: 9½ in. (24.5 cm)

YOU WILL NEED
- 1 x 50 g (approx 1¾ oz.) ball of Coats Regia Multi Color 4-ply, shade 5295
- set of size US 2 (2¾ mm) double-pointed needles
- two short lengths of smooth, contrasting yarn

GAUGE
30 sts and 42 rows to 4 in. (10 cm) over st-st on size 2 (2¾ mm) needles. Change needle size, if necessary, to obtain this gauge.

ABBREVIATIONS
k = knit; **st(s)** = stitch(es); **st-st** = stockinette stitch.

ABOUT THIS YARN
This smooth 75% wool, 25% polyamide, super-fine yarn is specially dyed to create bands of patterning alternating with stripes of color when knitted. Each 50 g (approx. 1¾ oz.) ball has about 230 yds. (210 m).

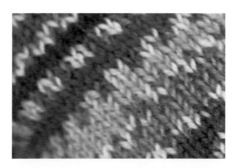

Skinny scarf

Once you know how to cast on, knit, purl, and bind off, you can knit almost anything—including this sophisticated scarf. It is simple and quick to create; why not knit one to match each of your favorite sweaters?

ESTIMATED TIME TO COMPLETE
This scarf was knitted in 2 hours.

ABOUT THIS YARN
Debbie Bliss Baby Alpaca Silk is a blend of 80% alpaca and 20% silk and has 75 yds. (65 m) to a 50 g (approx. 1¾ oz.) ball. It's usually knitted to an Aran-weight gauge, but larger needles make a soft, sensuous fabric.

SIZE
Width: 4¼ in. (11 cm); **length:** 57 in. (145 cm).

YOU WILL NEED
- 2 x 50 g balls (approx. 3½ oz.) of Debbie Bliss Baby Alpaca Silk in shade 04
- pair of size US 10 (6 mm) knitting needles

GAUGE
16 sts and 16 rows to 4 in. (10 cm) over st-st, when pressed, on size US 10 (6 mm) needles. Change needle size, if necessary, to obtain this gauge.

ABBREVIATIONS
k = knit; **p** = purl; **RS** = right side; **st(s)** = stitch(es); **st-st** = stockinette stitch.

SCARF
Cast on 18 sts.
Row 1 (RS) K.
Row 2 K2, p14, k2.
These 2 rows form st-st with k2 edgings.
Work until scarf measures 57 in. (145 cm). Bind off.

TO FINISH
Press according to yarn ball band. Weave in yarn ends.

TIPS

● For the neatest edge, join in the second ball of yarn on a wrong-side row, either just after the k2 at the beginning or just before the k2 at the end of the row. Don't knot the ends; just cross them over once, then weave them in on the wrong side, parallel with the edge of the scarf.

● You can bind off in the usual way, in which case you should finish with a knit row, so that the bound-off edge shows along the purl edge instead of the chain edge. Alternatively, you can use the following method of binding off, which mimics the cast-on edge almost exactly. Finish the knitting with a pattern Row 2. Thread a tapestry needle with the end of the yarn. Hold knitting needle with stitches in your left hand; insert needle with yarn purlwise through the first stitch; pull yarn through, and take needle around edge to back of work again. * Insert needle purlwise into second stitch, pull through, insert needle knitwise into first stitch, pull yarn through, and slip first stitch off needle. Tensioning the yarn to keep the edge neat, repeat from * until all stitches have been bound off. Weave in yarn end.

● If you want to speed up your knitting, try the fixed-needle method. Simply support the end of the right needle by tucking it firmly under your arm, then hold the right hand with the yarn above the needle. The right hand is then free to act like a shuttle, wrapping the yarn to make the stitches, with only the occasional pressure of the thumb needed to slide the stitches away from the point. Long needles are more comfortable for working this way.

Long and skinny, this scarf is stylish yet really simple to knit.

Fair Isle earflap hat

Working Fair Isle in rounds is so easy. Because the right side of the work is always facing, you see exactly where you are in the pattern. And because every round is knitted, it's definitely faster than working in rows.

ESTIMATED TIME TO COMPLETE
The hat took around 5 hours from start to finish, including the ends. Note: beginners new to this technique may take longer to complete this project.

ABOUT THIS YARN
Use pure wool or wool-rich-mix DK-weight yarns for this project. You'll find that differences in thickness between brands and yarns with different fiber mixes will not be apparent in Fair Isle. Check that the yarns you use can all be washed in the same way. If in doubt, wash it by hand.

SIZES
Measurement around head: 21½ [**23½**] in. (55[**60**] cm). Figures in square brackets refer to larger sizes; where there is one figure, it refers to both sizes.

YOU WILL NEED
- approximately 120 [**150**] g (4½ [**5½**] oz.) of wool and wool-mix DK-weight yarn; around 70 [**85**] g (2½ [**3**] oz.) of this should be in the main color (A) and 50 [**65**] g (2[**2½**] oz.) in contrasting colors (B)
- size US 6 (4 mm) circular needle, 24-in. (61-cm) long
- set of size US 6 (4 mm) double-pointed needles
- size US 3 (3¼ mm) circular needle, 32-in. (81-cm) long

GAUGE
24 sts and 26 rows to 4 in. (10 cm) over Fair Isle patt on size US 6 (4 mm) needles. Change needle size, if necessary, to obtain this gauge.

ABBREVIATIONS
cont = continue **dec** = decrease; **k** = knit; **patt** = pattern; **p** = purl; **rep** = repeat; **RS** = right side; **skpo** = slip 1, k1, pass slipped st over; **st(s)** = stitch(es); **tog** = together; **WS** = wrong side; **[ ]** = work instructions in square brackets as directed.

NOTES
- To work from chart in rounds, knit, reading every round from right to left. Instructions are also given for working from the chart in rows for the earflaps.
- Strand yarn not in use loosely on WS.
- The chart does not show any changes of color in the contrasting color (B). Change these B colors whenever you wish.
- The hat in the picture uses black as the main color (A) with 2 shades of green, a yellow, and 3 shades of pink and purple as the contrast colors (B).

TIPS

- When working Fair Isle patterns, spread out the stitches on the right needle each time you change color. This will stop the color rounds from pulling in.

- Save time at the end by knitting the yarn ends in over stitches of the same color on the next round.

- For the neatest results, always strand the yarns in the same order, keeping either the A yarn or the B yarn on top each time you change colors. It doesn't matter which way you do it, so long as you're always consistent.

- Because the hat is worked in the round, with every round knitted and only two colors in use at any one time, it's the ideal project to try working with one yarn in each hand. Hold the A yarn in your left hand and the B yarn in your right hand. Tension the A yarn around the pinky finger and over the middle finger. When knitting A stitches, take the right needle over the yarn and dip the tip to pull a loop through. Knit B stitches in the usual way.

Keep your head warm in style
with this sassy scrap-yarn hat.

colors for B whenever you desire, and work 34 more rounds from chart. Beg with 8th line of chart, patt 20 rounds.

Dec Round 1 Using A, [k9(**10**), k2tog] 12 times. 120(**132**) sts. Beg with first line of chart, patt 7 rounds.

Cont in A, K 1 round.

Dec Round 2 [K8(**9**), k2tog] 12 times. 108(**120**) sts.

K 1 round.

Dec Round 3 [K7(**8**), k2tog] 12 times. 96(**108**) sts.

K 1 round.

Dec Round 4 [K6(**7**), k2tog] 12 times. 84(**96**) sts.

K 1 round.

Dec Round 5 [K5(**6**), k2tog] 12 times. 72(**84**) sts.

K 1 round.

Dec Round 6 [K4(**5**), k2tog] 12 times. 60(**72**) sts.

K 1 round.

Dec Round 7 [K3(**4**), k2tog] 12 times. 48(**60**) sts.

K 1 round.

Dec Round 8 [K2(**3**), k2tog] 12 times. 36(**48**) sts.

K 1 round.

Dec Round 9 [K1(**2**), k2tog] 12 times. 24(**36**) sts.

K 1 round.

2nd size only, dec round 10 [K1, k2tog] 12 times.

K 1 round.

Both sizes 24 sts.

Next round [K2tog] 12 times. 12 sts.

K 1 round.

Next round [K2tog] 6 times. 6 sts. Leaving a long end, cut yarn. Thread end through sts, draw up, and secure top of hat.

CROWN

Using US 6 (4 mm) circular needle and A, cast on 132(**144**) sts. K 1 round. Work in patt from chart at right on page 31, changing to double-pointed needles when necessary.

Round 1 Omit edge st, rep 12 sts of first line of chart 11(**12**) times.

This round sets chart patt.

Cont in patt from chart, changing

EARFLAPS

Worked in rows, using two of the double-pointed needles.

Right earflap. Using A and with RS facing, skip 17(**20**) sts from start of round 1 and pick up 17 sts from next 17 sts of cast-on edge of hat.
P 1 row.
Work in patt from chart, as follows:

Row 1 (RS) K2A, reading 14th line of chart as a k row from right to left, work edge st and 12 sts of repeat, k2A.

Row 2 P2A, reading 15th line of chart as a p row, work 12 sts of repeat and edge st, p2A.

These 2 rows set chart patt in rows. Cont in patt, work 7 more rows.
P 1 row.

Dec row (RS) K1, [k2tog] twice, k to last 5 sts, [skpo] twice, k1. 13 sts.
P 1 row. Work dec row again. 9 sts.
P 1 row. Bind off.

Left earflap. Leave center 65(**71**) sts and pick up 17 sts from next 17 sts. Complete as given for right earflap.

EDGING

Using US 3 (3¼ mm) needle and A, with RS facing, beg at start of Round 1 of hat, pick up 17(**20**) sts to right earflap, 29 sts around earflap, 65(**71**) sts to left earflap, 29 sts around left earflap and 16(**19**) sts to beg of round. 156(**168**) sts.

Round 1 [P1, k1] to end.
This round forms rib. Rib 3 more rounds. Turn the work and bind off loosely purlwise.

TO FINISH

Weave in yarn ends. Press hat. Make a 5-in. (13-cm) tassel in one of the B shades and sew on top of hat, as shown in the photo at left.

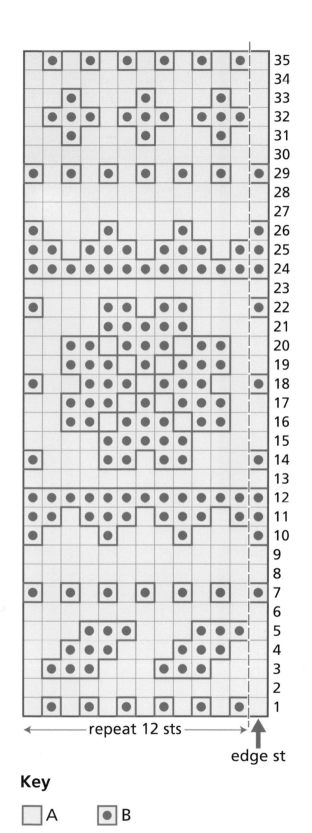

← repeat 12 sts →

edge st

Key

☐ A   ▣ B

Fair Isle fingerless gloves

Like the Fair Isle hat (see pages 28–31), these gloves are worked in the round, so you just knit every row. You can try the gloves on as you work to check the fit; because they're seamless, they're extra-comfortable.

ESTIMATED TIME TO COMPLETE
Each glove took around 2 hours to knit: 4 hours total for the pair.

ABOUT THIS YARN
Use any combination of pure wool or wool-rich-mix DK-weight yarns for this project. Just check that the yarns you use can all be washed in the same way. If in doubt, wash your gloves by hand.

SIZE
Measurement around hand: 8 in. (20 cm). These gloves will fit an average woman's hands.

YOU WILL NEED
- 60 g (approx. 2¼ oz.) of wool and wool-mix DK-weight yarn; 40 g (approx. 1½ oz.) of this should be in the main color (A) and 20 g (¾ oz.) in contrasting colors (B)
- set each of size US 3 (3¼ mm) and size US 6 (4 mm) double-pointed needles

GAUGE
24 sts and 26 rows to 4 in. (10 cm) over Fair Isle patt on size US 6 (4 mm) needles. Change needle size, if necessary, to obtain this gauge.

ABBREVIATIONS
beg = begin(ning); **cont** = continue; **dp** = double-pointed; **foll** = following; **k** = knit; **patt** = pattern; **p** = purl; **rep** = repeat; **RS** = right side; **skpo** = slip 1, k1, pass slipped st over; **st(s)** = stitch(es); **tog** = together; **WS** = wrong side; **[ ]** = work instructions in square brackets as directed.

NOTES
- The gloves use the same chart as the hat (see page 31).
- To work from chart in rounds, k, reading every round from right to left.
- Strand yarn not in use loosely on WS.
- The chart does not show any changes of color in the contrasting yarn (B). Change these colors whenever you wish.
- The gloves in the photo at right, above use some of the same colors as the hat, but you could use any combination of colors you like.
- If you are working with a set of 4 double-pointed needles, divide the 48 stitches by 3, and put 16 sts on each of 3 needles; if you have a set of 5 needles, put 12 stitches on each of 4 needles for the main part of the gloves.
- For clarity, the number of stitches for each of 3 needles is given in the instructions for working the fingers.

GLOVES

Left glove. Using smaller needles and A, cast on 48 sts.
Round 1 [K2, p2] to end.
This round forms ribbing. Rib 11 more rounds.
Change to larger needles. K 1 round.
Work in patt from chart, as follows:
Round 1 Omit edge st, work 12 sts of first line of chart 4 times.
This round sets chart patt.
Cont in patt from chart changing colors for B whenever desired, work 21 more rounds from chart.
Thumb-opening round Using A, k1, slip next 9 sts onto a holder and cast on in A 9 sts in their place, k38. This round corresponds to 23rd line of chart. Beg with 24th line of chart, patt 12 rounds from chart.
Cont in A. K 2 rounds **.
1st finger K first 3 sts of round and leave these 3 sts on a holder; using first dp needle, k next 6 st; using 2nd dp needle, k foll 6 sts; using 3rd dp needle, k next 3 sts, cast on 3 sts, leave remaining 30 sts on a holder. 18 sts. Join in a round and k next 3 rounds from chart. Bind off purlwise.
2nd finger Slip 3 sts knitted at beg onto first dp needle, then pick up 3

Keep your hands warm and colorful with these nifty fingerless gloves.

sts from cast-on sts of first finger; using 2nd needle, k next 6 sts from holder; using 3rd needle, cast on 3 sts; slip last 3 sts from holder onto spare needle and k these 3 sts. 18 sts. Complete as first finger.

3rd finger Using first needle, pick up 3 sts from cast-on sts of 2nd finger; k next 3 sts from holder; using 2nd needle, k next 2 sts from holder; cast on 3 sts; slip last 5 sts from holder onto spare needle; using 3rd needle, k these 5 sts. 16 sts. Complete as first finger.

4th finger Using first needle, pick up 3 sts from cast-on sts of 3rd finger; k next 2 sts from holder; using 2nd needle, k foll 4 sts from holder; using 3rd needle, k last 5 sts from holder. 14 sts. Complete as first finger.

Thumb Using first needle, k9 from holder; using 2nd needle, pick up 1 st from row end and 4 sts from cast-on sts; using 3rd needle, pick up 5 sts from cast-on sts and 1 st from row end. 20 sts. K 5 rounds from chart. Bind off purlwise.

Right glove. Work as left glove to **.

4th finger K first 18 sts of round and leave these 18 sts on a holder. Using first needle, k next 5 sts; using 2nd needle, k foll 4 sts; using 3rd needle, k next 2 sts; cast on 3 sts; leave 19 sts on second holder. 14 sts. K 3 rounds. Bind off purlwise.

3rd finger Using first needle, pick up 3 sts from cast-on sts of 4th finger; k2 sts from holder; using 2nd needle, k next 3 sts from holder; cast on 3 sts; slip last 5 sts from

holder at beg onto spare needle; using 3rd needle, k these 5 sts. 16 sts. Complete as 4th finger.

2nd finger Slip 3 sts knitted at beg onto first needle; then pick up 3 sts from cast-on sts of 2nd finger; using 2nd needle, k next 6 sts from holder; using 3rd needle, cast on 3 sts; slip last 3 sts from holder at beg onto spare needle and k these 3 sts. 18 sts. Complete as 4th finger.

1st finger Using first needle, k next 6 sts; using 2nd needle, k foll 6 sts; using 3rd needle, k last 3 sts; pick up 3 sts from cast-on sts of 3rd finger. 18 sts. Complete as 4th finger.

Right thumb Work as for left thumb.

TO FINISH
Weave in yarn ends. Press.

Floppy-brim hat

The brim of this hat is knitted first, in garter stitch; then the stitches are picked up and the crown worked in stockinette stitch. The brim is shaped by knitting part of a row, then turning the work and knitting back. Each time, the number of stitches to work and the number left after turning are given. Don't be put off by the "yf"s and "yb"s; this just means bringing the yarn to the front of the work as if to purl, slipping a stitch, and taking the yarn to the back of the work again to anchor it around the stitch.

ESTIMATED TIME TO COMPLETE
The hat took around 13 hours; finishing up and making the flower took 1 additional hour: 14 hours total.

ABOUT THIS YARN
Rowan Yorkshire Tweed DK is a 100% pure new wool yarn with approximately 123 yds. (113 m) to a 50 g (approx 1¾ oz.) ball. It is made from two softly twisted strands plied together and has little flecks in several shades contrasting with the main color.

SIZE
Around head: 22 in. (56 cm). This hat will fit an average woman's head.

YOU WILL NEED
• 3 x 50 g balls (approx 1¾ oz.) of Rowan Yorkshire Tweed DK in Revel, shade 342
• pair of size US 3 (3¼ mm) knitting needles

GAUGE
23 sts and 38 rows to 4 in. (10 cm) over gst on size US 3 (3¼ mm) needles. Change needle size, if necessary, to obtain this gauge.

ABBREVIATIONS
beg = beginning; **dec** = decrease; **gst** = garter st; **k** = knit; **kfb** = k into front and back of st; **p** = purl; **RS** = right side; **skpo** = slip 1, k1, pass slip st over; **sl** = slip; **st(s)** = stitch(es); **st-st** = stockinette st; **tog** = together; **yb** = yarn to back of work; **yf** = yarn to front of work; **[ ]** = work instructions in square brackets as directed.

NOTES
• The gauge for the hat is tighter than usual for Yorkshire Tweed DK, because the hat fabric needs to be firm.
• Working yf before and yb after the slipped stitch anchors the yarn around the stitch and closes the hole made by turning the work.
• It's easier to count the number of sections in the brim if you mark each group of 12 turning rows.

BRIM
Cast on 40 sts.
Rows 1 and 2 K40.
Row 3 K22, yf, sl 1, yb, turn and leave 17 sts.
Row 4 Sl 1, yb, k22.
Rows 5 and 6 K40.
Row 7 K12, yf, sl 1, yb, turn and leave 27 sts.
Row 8 Sl 1, yb, k12.
Rows 9 and 10 K40.
Row 11 K22, yf, sl 1, yb, turn and leave 17 sts.
Row 12 Sl 1, yb, k22.
Work these 12 rows 28 more times. K 2 rows. Bind off.

CROWN
Pick up 130 sts from short edge of brim. Beg p row, st-st 25 rows.
Shape top. Dec Row 1 (RS) K1, [k2tog, k12, skpo] 8 times, k1. 114 sts. St-st 7 rows.
Dec Row 2 K1, [k2tog, k10, skpo] 8 times, k1. 98 sts. St-st 5 rows.
Dec Row 3 K1, [k2tog, k8, skpo] 8 times, k1. 82 sts. St-st 5 rows.
Dec Row 4 K1, [k2tog, k6, skpo] 8 times, k1. 66 sts. St-st 3 rows.
Dec Row 5 K1, [k2tog, k4, skpo] 8 times, k1. 50 sts. St-st 3 rows.
Dec Row 6 K1, [k2tog, k2, skpo] 8

times, k1. 34 sts. P 1 row.

Dec Row 7 K1, [k2tog, skpo] 8
times, k1. 18 sts. P 1 row.

Dec Row 8 K1, [k2tog, skpo] 4
times, k1. 10 sts. P 1 row.
Leaving a long end, cut yarn. Thread
end through sts at top of hat, draw
up, and secure.

FLOWER

Picot-ring center. Make a slip knot
on left needle. Using two needles,
[cast on 3 sts, bind off 3 sts] 5
times, pick up and k 1 st from first st
and bind off 1 st, so leaving 1 st on
needle. Transfer this st to left
needle.

1st petal Cast on 1 st. 2 sts.

Row 1 K1, kfb. 3 sts.

Row 2 K3.

Row 3 K2, kfb. 4 sts.

Row 4 K4.

Row 5 K3, kfb. 5 sts.

Rows 6, 7, 8, and 9 K.

Row 10 K2tog, k3. 4 sts.

Row 11 K4.

Row 12 K2tog, k2. 3 sts.

Row 13 K3.

Row 14 K2tog, k1.

Row 15 K2.

Row 16 K2tog.

One st on right needle. Pick up and k
1 st from between next 2 picots and
bind off 1 st.

Transfer remaining st to left needle
and work 4 more petals in this way.
Fasten off. For a bigger flower,
simply work another round of petals.

Firm knitting in pure wool gives an
almost felted, sculptural quality to
this dramatic hat.

TO FINISH

Join back seam of crown and brim
of hat. Fold 11 rows just before start
of shaping in half and sew to make a
tuck, enclosing strands of spare yarn
to stiffen the tuck. Fold up brim and
sew on flower. Weave in yarn ends.

Rainbow scarf

Beginners will find this scarf is an ideal learn-to-knit project. Working in rib stripes is great for practicing both knit and purl, and it helps the work grow quickly. Experienced knitters will appreciate the opportunity to use up leftover yarns. Leave long yarn ends; then knot and trim the ends to make a fringe along one long edge of the scarf.

ESTIMATED TIME TO COMPLETE
The scarf took 14 hours to knit.

SIZE
Width: 6 in. (15 cm) excluding tassels; **length:** 63 in. (160 cm).

YOU WILL NEED
- 250 g (approx. 9 oz.) total weight of wool or wool mix-DK in as many shades as you can find of pink, red, orange, yellow, green, blue (including indigo), and purple.
- pair of size US 5 (3¾ mm) knitting needles

GAUGE
26 sts and 26 rows to 4 in. (10 cm) over rib, when pressed, on size US 5 (3¾ mm) needles. Change needle size, if necessary, to obtain this gauge.

ABBREVIATIONS
cont = continue; **k** = knit; **patt** = pattern; **p** = purl; **RS** = right side; **st(s)** = stitch(es); **[ ]** = work instructions in square brackets as directed.

NOTES
- Each 4-row stripe uses 2 shades of each color, changed at random for each 28-row repeat.
- Use as many shades of each color as you can find. Sort the yarns into the 7 color groups and select a different shade for each two-row stripe.
- When changing colors, leave ends of around 6 in. (15 cm).

SCARF
Using green, cast on 40 sts. K2 rows.
Row 1 (RS) K3, [p4, k2] to last st, k1.
Row 2 P3, [k4, p2] to last st, p1.

These 2 rows form rib.
Cont in rib, working 2 more rows in another shade of green, then work:
2 rows in yellow, 2 rows in another shade of yellow,
2 rows in orange, 2 rows in another shade of orange,
2 rows in red, 2 rows in another shade of red,
2 rows in pink, 2 rows in another shade of pink,
2 rows in purple, 2 rows in another shade of purple,
2 rows in indigo, 2 rows in blue,
2 rows in green, 2 rows in another shade of green.
These 28 rows form the patt.
Changing shades with each repeat, as desired, cont until scarf measures 63 in. (160 cm). Cont in same color as last stripe, k 1 row.
Bind off knitwise.

TO FINISH
For each tassel, cut an 8-in. (20-cm) length of yarn in an appropriate color. Make a slip knot in the center. Take 4 ends of yarn from the edge of the scarf, slide the slip knot over the ends and up close to the edge of the scarf. Tighten the knot; then using all 6 ends, tie an overhand knot close to the edge of the scarf to make a tassel. Repeat until all ends are secured. Trim the tassels to the same length. Press scarf.

TIPS

● Although DK-weight yarns from different sources are theoretically the same, the actual thickness will vary from brand to brand. In a project like this, slight variations in thickness won't matter.

● It is essential to use yarns with the same or similar fiber content. Wool and wool-mix yarns are suggested, so the scarf can be pressed to open out the rib.

● You could work the scarf in stripes just two colors, but remember to cut the yarn, leaving a long end each time you change colors to make the fringe.

If you don't have all the colors, swap yarns with friends or use a hank of tapestry yarn.

Braided scarf

Braiding with five strands of yarn is as simple as making an ordinary three-strand braid, but the result is firmer and fatter. Once you've organized the strands of yarn, the braiding is quick and easy.

ESTIMATED TIME TO COMPLETE
The scarf took 2 hours to make.

ABOUT THIS YARN
Sirdar Denim Ultra is a super-thick, soft, lightweight yarn. It's a mix of 60% acrylic, 25% cotton, and 15% wool and has 82 yds. (75 m) to a 100 g (approx. 3½ oz.) ball.

SIZE
Length: 118 in. (approx. 3¼ yds. [300 cm])

YOU WILL NEED
• 5 x 100 g balls (approx. 17½ oz.) of Sirdar Denim Ultra in Ivory Cream, shade 508.
• a frame (see Notes below) on which to make the braid.

NOTES
• The back of a slatted wooden chair would make an ideal frame. Tie each strand of the braid to a different strut to keep them spaced evenly.
• The braid is made of 5 strands, and you've got only two hands. It will really speed up the work if you can get two friends to hold 2 of the strands each while you manipulate the fifth strand, exchanging strands as you complete each step.

TIPS

● Place a rubber band around each prepared ball of strands to prevent it from unwinding. Slip the band off as required to release more of the strand.

● If there's no one handy to help with the braiding, keep the prepared balls of yarn separate by placing each one in a box or plastic bag, so they don't roll around and get tangled.

● Use clothespins to hold the strands of yarn together as you braid.

PREPARATION
Cut 12 lengths of yarn, each 6½ yds. (6 m) long, from one ball of yarn. Line up strands, tie a short length of spare yarn firmly around them, a little way down from one end, and knot this end of the strands around frame or chair back. Comb down the length of the strands with your fingers to smooth them out; then wind them into a ball to keep them neat until needed. Repeat with each of the other 4 balls of yarn, knotting the tied ends to adjacent struts of the frame.

BRAIDING

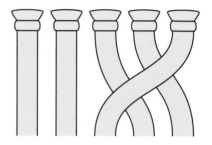

Step 1 Take the far-right strand over the next 2 strands to the center.
Step 2 Take the far-left strand over the next 2 strands to the center.

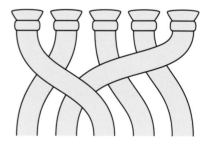

Repeat these 2 steps, tensioning the strands each time to make a fat braid. Continue until almost all of the yarn has been braided. Using spare yarn, tie the yarn ends of each of the 5 strands together; then bind the 5 strands together with spare yarn, knotting it securely. Trim strand ends to make a tassel. Undo the strands from the frame, and finish the other end of the braid in the same way.

This must be the simplest scarf ever! It's just a big fat braid of soft cotton-mix yarn.

Pom-pom scarf

Enjoy the feel of the yarn as you wind the pom-poms, then link them together and pop your scarf on! You can use up any spare scraps for this project, though thicker yarn makes pom-poms faster.

ESTIMATED TIME TO COMPLETE
It takes 20 minutes to make each of the 10 pom-poms: 3 hours and 20 minutes total, plus around 50 minutes total.

ABOUT THIS YARN
You can use almost any yarn to make pom-poms. The scarf in the photo at right was made using smooth 4-ply, DK, and Aran-weight (worsted-weight) yarns in a variety of colors.

SIZE
Pom-pom: 3 in. (8 cm) in diameter; **length:** 46 in. (117 cm).

YOU WILL NEED
- assorted yarns in varying weights
- pom-pom template (see below) and cardboard
- sharp scissors
- large tapestry needle
- large, sharp darning needle

NOTE
• You can buy plastic pom-pom rings or make two of your own cardboard rings from the template given below.

TIPS

● Two lids from family-size tubs of yogurt make good pom-pom templates. Cut a hole in the center of one lid, then trace the hole onto another lid so that the holes will match.

● If you want a wider scarf, make more pom-poms and join them in pairs as well as in a length.

● If you want multi-colored pom-poms, just change color when winding the yarn around the template.

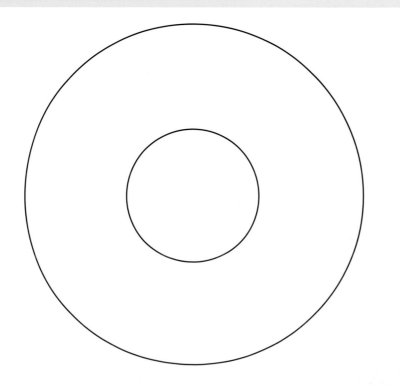

Pom-pom template
Trace template. Transfer to stiff cardboard, and cut 2 rings with holes in the center.

POM-POMS

Place the 2 rings together. Using yarn of your choice threaded double in the tapestry needle, wrap yarn around pom-pom template until the hole is thickly packed. Have a 30-in. (76-cm) length of spare yarn ready. Insert scissors between rings, and cut through yarn around entire edge. Slide the center of the length of spare yarn between the rings, wrap tightly around the center of the pom-pom, and knot it firmly, leaving 2 long ends of spare yarn. Remove pom-pom rings. Trim pom-pom, but do not cut off the long ends. Make 9 more pom-poms.

TO FINISH

Thread the darning needle with the 2 ends of the first pom-pom. Insert needle in second pom-pom opposite the long ends, and pull through until around 1½ in. (4 cm) of yarn is left between pom-poms. Take needle back through second pom-pom and knot yarn; then take needle back through first pom-pom to beginning and through again to knot yarn. Trim ends. Join each pom-pom in this way until all 10 pom-poms have been joined. Trim ends of last pom-pom.

Use scraps of thick yarn to create this fun scarf.

Scattered-sequin scarf

This scarf is just a long length of knitting in stockinette stitch, with borders in garter stitch. The sequins are sewn on afterward, using tiny beads to hold them in place so the stitching is hidden. The yarn is beautifully soft, with the luxurious touch of cashmere, and the scarf will be a joy to wear, with or without the sequins.

ESTIMATED TIME TO COMPLETE
The scarf took 10 hours to knit, plus 1 hour to sew on the sequins.

ABOUT THIS YARN
Debbie Bliss Cashmerino Aran is a soft, supple yarn that's a mix of 55% merino wool, 33% microfiber, and 12% cashmere. It has approximately 100 yds. (90 m) to a 50 g (approx. 1¾ oz.) ball. Cashmerino Aran is available in brilliant jewel shades, soft pastels, naturals, and rich, dark colors.

SIZE
Width: 11 in. (28 cm); **length:** 75 in. (190 cm)

YOU WILL NEED
- 6 x 50 g balls (approx. 10½ oz.) of Debbie Bliss Cashmerino Aran in shade 615
- pair each of size US 7 (4½ mm) and size US 8 (5mm) knitting needles
- large sequins and tiny beads
- matching sewing thread and a fine, sharp sewing needle

GAUGE
18 sts and 24 rows to 4 in. (10 cm) over st-st on size US 8 (5 mm) needles. Change needle size, if necessary, to obtain this gauge.

ABBREVIATIONS
beg = beginning; **cont** = continue; **k** = knit; **p** = purl; **RS** = right side; **st(s)** = stitch(es); **st-st** = stockinette st; **WS** = wrong side.

NOTE
- It's easier to hide the woven-in ends if you always join in a new ball of yarn on the inner edge of the k2 edging.

Add a touch of glitter to an exquisitely soft, generously sized scarf.

SCARF
Using size US 7 (4½ mm) needles, cast on 50 sts. K 4 rows.
Change to size US 8 (5 mm) needles.
Row 1 (RS) K.
Row 2 K2, p to last 2 sts, k2.
These 2 rows form st-st with k2 edgings.

Work straight until scarf measures 74 in. (188 cm), ending with Row 2. Change to US 7 (4½ mm) needles. K 5 rows. Bind off knitwise.

TO FINISH
Weave in ends. Press according to yarn ball band.

TO DECORATE Sequins are placed randomly on each end of the scarf. To sew on sequins neatly, first make a couple of tiny stitches on the right side to secure the thread; bring the needle up through the hole in the sequin and then through a tiny bead, then over the bead and back down through the sequin hole and the scarf. If you're placing a sequin on the wrong side of the scarf as well, do the same with a second sequin and bead; then stitch behind the sequin to bring needle out ready to sew through and secure the other holes with beads in the same way before fastening off with backstitch on the wrong side of the scarf.

TIPS

● If you prefer to count the rows rather than measure your scarf, you'll need to work 450 rows in st-st with k2 edgings.

● Save time at the end by weaving in the ends as you work, using a tapestry needle and threading the ends through the row ends on the reverse-stockinette-stitch side of the scarf.

● You can use any size sequins that you like, either matching them to the yarn color, or choosing colors to go with the rest of your outfit. If the sequins are smaller, just add more of them. If the sequins have only one hole, either in the center or at the top, you can still sew them on, using beads to hide the stitching.

● The sequins in the photos at right have a hole at the top and the bottom. Now widely available, you can choose from a range of metallic and pearlized finishes to match your yarn.

● Do not press sequins; they will curl. Press your scarf on the reverse side.

Leg warmers

There's no need to purl when you work stockinette stitch in the round—and no need to sew seams, either. These leg warmers are perfect for yoga or for filling in the chilly gaps at the tops of your boots.

ESTIMATED TIME TO COMPLETE
The leg warmers took 4 hours each to make—a total of 8 hours for the pair.

SIZE
Circumference: 12 in. (30.5 cm); **length:** approx. 16 in. (40.5 cm).

YOU WILL NEED
- 2 x 50 g balls (approx. 3½ oz.) of Regia Multi-Color 6-ply in Passion, shade 0540
- Set of size US 5 (3¾ mm) double-pointed needles

GAUGE
22 sts and 30 rows to 4 in. (10 cm) over st-st on size US 5 (3¾ mm) needles. Change needle size, if necessary, to obtain this gauge.

ABBREVIATIONS
k = knit; **st(s)** = stitch(es); **st-st** = stockinette st.

NOTE
- If using four double-pointed needles, arrange 22 sts on each of 3 needles and knit with the fourth needle. If your set has 5 needles put 16 sts on each of 2 needles and 17 stitches on each of 2 more needles, knit with the fifth needle.

TIPS

- These leg warmers are very stretchy, so you can pull them up or push them down to wear them however you want.

- If the second ball of yarn, for the second leg warmer, doesn't start in the same place in the color sequence as the first ball, wind off the yarn until you get to the right color, then add the spare yarn at the top, so the stripes of color match.

- If you prefer, you could knit the leg warmers using a short circular needle.

LEG WARMERS
Cast on 22 sts on each of 3 needles. Taking care not to twist sts on the needles, join in a round and k every round for st-st until almost all of one ball of yarn has been used. Bind off. Repeat for second leg warmer. Weave in yarn ends.

ABOUT THIS YARN
Regia 6-ply is a hard-wearing DK-weight 75% wool, 25% polyamide yarn, which has approximately 136 yds. (125 m) to a 50 g (approx. 1¾ oz.) ball. It is dyed in bursts of color to give a random, striped effect.

Stripes appear like
magic as you knit these
fun leg warmers.

Leopard-spotted headband

The texture of the yarn gives the leopard-spotted motifs in this headband a fabulous furry look. And if you miss a stitch when following the chart, the effect will be more authentic—no two spots on an animal are ever the same!

ESTIMATED TIME TO COMPLETE
The headband took 4 hours to knit, and 5 minutes to finish.

ABOUT THIS YARN
Patons Whisper has long, soft filaments trapped in a chain construction yarn to give a faux-fur effect. It's 100% polyester and has 98 yds. (90 m) to a 50 g (approx. 1¾ oz.) ball.

SIZE
This adjustable headband will fit an average woman's head.

YOU WILL NEED
* 1 x 50 g ball (approx. 1¾ oz.) of Patons Whisper in Wicker, shade 00011 (A), and Jet, shade 00007 (B)
* pair of size US 6 (4¼ mm) knitting needles
* 8 in. (20 cm) ½-in. (1.5-cm) wide soft elastic

GAUGE
22 sts and 30 rows to 4 in. (10 cm) over motif patt in st-st on size US 6 (4 mm) needles. Change needle size, if necessary, to obtain this gauge.

ABBREVIATIONS
beg = beginning; **cont** = continue; **k** = knit; **patt** = pattern; **p** = purl; **RS** = right side; **st(s)** = stitch(es); **st-st** = stockinette stitch; **WS** = wrong side.

NOTES
* To work from chart, read first and every RS (k) row from right to left, 2nd and every WS (p) row from left to right.
* Use separate small amounts of yarn wound on bobbins for motifs in B and areas in A between motifs.
* Twist yarns when changing colors to link areas.

HEADBAND
Using A, cast on 27 sts. Beg with a k row, st-st 6 rows.
Work in patt from chart for 37 rows.
Cont in A, st-st 5 rows.
Work 37 rows in patt from chart.
Cont in A, st-st 9 rows.
Bind off knitwise.

TO FINISH
Gather cast-on and cast-off ends. Thread elastic through gathered ends of headband, adjust to fit, trimming elastic if necessary, and secure ends.

TIPS

● When working the motifs, wind yarn off onto bobbins for larger areas; just use lengths of yarn for smaller areas.

● Deal with the ends as you work by knitting them in over stitches of the same color in the next row; the hairs in the yarn will lock the ends in place after just a few stitches. At the end, check that the ends are secure and trim off any excess yarn.

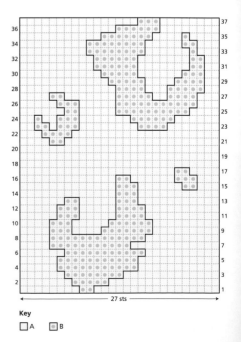

27 sts

Key
☐ A ▨ B

Add a touch of glamour to any outfit with this animal-print headband.

Simple stitches and rapid progress make this wrap the ideal project to create on the move. You'll be surprised what you can achieve in spare moments, even while traveling.

Tassel wrap

This flamboyant knit is a cross between a wrap and a poncho. Wear it like a shawl, trail the ends down your back, or wrap it asymmetrically for a fashion look that keeps you warm.

ESTIMATED TIME TO COMPLETE
The wrap took 8 hours to knit.

SIZE
Width: (at widest point) 43 in. (109 cm); **length:** 41½ in. (106 cm).

YOU WILL NEED
- 9 x 100 g balls (approx. 32 oz.) of Rowan Biggy Print in pink, shade 237
- pair of size US 35 (20 mm) knitting needles
- size US M 13 (9.00 mm) crochet hook

GAUGE
5½ sts and 7 rows to 4 in. (10 cm) over st-st on size US 35 (20 mm) needles. Change needle size, if necessary, to obtain this gauge.

ABBREVIATIONS
beg = beginning; **cont** = continue; **dec** = decrease; **k** = knit; **kfb** = k into front and back of st; **p** = purl; **pfb** = p into front and back of st; **RS** = right side; **skpo** = slip 1, k1, pass slip st over; **st(s)** = stitch(es); **st-st** = stockinette st; **tog** = together; **yo** = yarn over needle to make a stitch.

NOTE
- Do not join in a new ball of yarn in the middle of a row; always join in at a side edge.

TO FINISH
Using a crochet hook and with WS facing, work a row of single crochet around edge of wrap. Using 7 x 15-in. (38-cm) lengths of yarn doubled for each tassel, plus a 28-in. (71-cm) length to tie the tassel, make 29 tassels. Sew a tassel on each point and 6 tassels on each of the 4 outer edges. Trim tassels to the same length.

ABOUT THIS YARN
Biggy Print is a soft and chunky 100% merino wool yarn made of 2 strands of varying thickness plied together. It has 33 yds. (30 m) to a 100 g (approx. 3½ oz.) ball.

TIP
- If you don't get the correct gauge, changing needles may not fix the problem, since there's a big jump between sizes in large needles. If you are only slightly off gauge, try tensioning the yarn around your fingers.

WRAP
Cast on 3 sts.
Row 1 (RS) Yo, k to last st, kfb. 5 sts.
Row 2 Yo, p to last st, pfb. 7 sts.
These 2 rows form st-st with incs at beg and end of rows.
Cont in st-st, inc in this way at each end of every row until there are 61 sts.
Shape neck. Next row (WS) P 29, bind off 3 sts knitwise, p to end.
Cont on first set of 29 sts for first side, leaving 29 sts for 2nd side.
1st side. Row 1 (RS) K1, k2tog, k23, skpo, p1. 27 sts.

Row 2 P.
Cont in st-st, dec in same way as Row 1 at each end of next 3 RS rows. 21 sts. Dec as set at beg of next 18 RS rows. 3 sts. Bind off knitwise. With RS facing join yarn at neck edge.
2nd side. Row 1 (RS) P1, k2tog, k23, skpo, k1. 27 sts.
Row 2 P.
Cont in st-st, dec in same way as Row 1 each end of next 3 RS rows. 21 sts. Dec as set at end of next 18 RS rows. 3 sts. Bind off knitwise.

This sophisticated ribbed cowl sits neatly over the shoulders. Wear it indoors over a little top or outdoors over a jacket.

Cream ribbed cowl

The cowl is worked entirely in the round, so there are no seams to spoil the surface of the rib pattern. Make the cowl in neutrals to go with all your outerwear, or pick a blending shade to match your favorite coat.

ESTIMATED TIME TO COMPLETE
The cowl took 6 hours to knit, and 2 minutes to weave in the ends.

ABOUT THIS YARN
Debbie Bliss Cashmerino Super-chunky is a substantial but deliciously soft mix of 55% merino wool, 33% microfiber, and 12% cashmere. There are 82 yds. (75 m) to a 100 g (approx. 3½ oz.) ball.

SIZE
Width: around lower edge: 45½ in. (116 cm); **length:** 8½ in. (22 cm) (excluding collar).

YOU WILL NEED
- 4 x 100 g balls (approx. 14 oz.) of Debbie Bliss Cashmerino Super-chunky in shade 01
- medium-length size US 10½ (7 mm) circular needle

GAUGE
12 sts and 18 rows to 4 in. (10 cm) over rib in the round, when pressed, on size 10½ (7 mm) circular needle. Change needle size, if necessary, to obtain this gauge.

ABBREVIATIONS
dec = decrease; **k** = knit; **p** = purl; **skpo** = slip one, k1, pass slipped st over; **st(s)** = stitch(es); **tog** = together; **[ ]** = work instructions in square brackets as directed.

TIPS

- Work your gauge swatch by knitting to and fro in the usual way.

- Working in the round makes knitting look neater, so your row gauge may be slightly tighter than when working flat pieces.

- Check carefully to make sure that the stitches are not twisted on the needle at the end of the first round. It can be easier to see the stitches on the needle if, after casting on, you turn and work the first round as a row, then join and continue in rounds.

- Store your work wrapped in a piece of white cotton cloth to keep it clean.

COWL
Cast on 140 sts. Work in rounds.
Round 1 (RS) [K2, p2] to end, joining sts into a round. This round forms rib. Rib 35 more rounds.
Dec Round 1 [K2, p1, k2tog, skpo, p1, k2, rib 10] 7 times. 126 sts.
Dec Round 2 [K2, k2tog, skpo, k2, rib 10] 7 times. 112 sts.
Dec Round 3 [K1, k2tog, skpo, k1, rib 10] 7 times. 98 sts.
Dec Round 4 [K2tog, skpo, rib 10] 7 times. 84 sts.
Collar. Rib 44 rounds. Bind off in rib.

TO FINISH
Press according to yarn ball band. Weave in the yarn ends.

Fizz wrap

Ideal for beginners, this wrap will keep you warm in style. Of course, a piece this size can't be knitted overnight, but you really could not find a simpler knit—just cast on and knit every row.

ESTIMATED TIME TO COMPLETE
The wrap took 35 hours to knit.

SIZE
Length: 63 in. (160 cm); **width:** 20 in. (50 cm).

YOU WILL NEED
- 9 x 50 g balls (approx. 16 oz.) of Sirdar New Fizz in Sapphire, shade 0798
- pair of size US 10½ (7 mm) knitting needles

GAUGE
14 sts and 18 rows to 4 in. (10 cm) over gst on size US 10½ (7 mm) needles Change needle size, if necessary, to obtain this gauge.

ABBREVIATIONS
k = knit; **gst** = garter stitch; **st(s)** = stitch(es)

WRAP
Cast on 70 sts.
K every row until wrap measures 63 in. (160 cm) long. Bind off.

TO FINISH
Weave in yarn ends.

TIPS

● The fabric is so flexible that the size of the wrap will change when it's held up or worn, so don't worry about the precise length. Just knit until almost all of the 9 balls of yarn have been used, then bind off.

● Inevitably, some of the yarn's tags and tassels will get snarled as you knit. Don't stop and pick them out—wait until you're working the next row; then use the tip of the right needle to flick out the trapped tag before knitting the next stitch. A good shake when you've finished the wrap will also release trapped ends.

ABOUT THIS YARN
Sirdar New Fizz has a smooth, firmly twisted core with contrasting tags of paper-look fabric and shiny tassels of yarn twisted in it. Its mix of 72% nylon, 19% acrylic, and 9% polyester makes a light, but deeply textured fabric. There are approx. 82 yds. (75 m) to a 50 g (approx. 1¾ oz.) ball.

VARIATION
Trimming a handbag with a narrow strip of this yarn, knitted as above, will create a matching accessory for the wrap.

For a special effect, decorate your wrap with beads and sequins, sewn to the ends with matching thread.

Comfort wrap

When is a wrap not a wrap? When it's an afghan! Super-thick yarn and giant needles make this a fast knit despite the size. Wear it as a comfort blanket or use it as a sofa throw.

ESTIMATED TIME TO COMPLETE
The wrap took 17 hours to knit.

SIZE
Width: 25 in. (63 cm); **length:** 67½ in. (172 cm).

YOU WILL NEED
- 12 x 100 g balls (approx. 42 oz.) of Sirdar Bigga in Cream, shade 685
- pair of size US 19 (15 mm) knitting needles
- cable needle

GAUGE
12 sts measure 5½ in. (14 cm), 9 rows to 4 in. (10 cm) over cable-and-rib patt on size US 19 (15 mm) needles. Change needle size, if necessary, to obtain this gauge.

ABBREVIATIONS
c6b = slip next 3 sts onto cable needle and hold at back of work; k3, k3 from cable needle; **cont** = continue; **k** = knit; **kfb** = k into front and back of st; **p** = purl; **patt** = pattern; **RS** = right side; **st(s)** = stitch(es); **tog** = together; **[ ]** = work instructions in square brackets as directed.

NOTES
- Do not join in yarn at edges; join new yarn 2 sts in from edge. This will make it easier to hide the woven-in ends.
- Increases behind the cables on Row 5 and decreases behind the cables on the fifth row from the end help to keep the edges flat.

TIPS

- If you can't find a fat cable needle, you could improvise by using a blunt pencil or an empty pen case. Or you could slip the stitches onto a stitch holder, then put them on the left needle to work.

- Tucking the right needle under your arm will help take the weight as the wrap gets bigger.

- If you prefer, you could use a circular size US 19 (15 mm) needle, working to and fro in the usual way. As the wrap grows, the weight will lie in your lap rather than hanging on the needles.

WRAP
Cast on 50 sts.
Row 1: (RS) K4, [p2, k5, p2, k2] 4 times, k2.
Row 2: K2, [p2, k2, p5, k2] 4 times, p2, k2.
Rows 3 and 4: As Rows 1 and 2.
Row 5: (RS) K4, [p2, slip next 2 sts onto cable needle, hold at back, k3, then work kfb, k1 from cable needle, p2, k2] 4 times, k2. 54 sts.
Row 6: K2, [p2, k2, p6, k2] 4 times, p2, k2.
Row 7: (RS) K4, [p2, k6, p2, k2] 4 times, k2.
Row 8: as Row 6.
Rows 9, 10, 11, and 12: As rows 7 and 8.
Row 13: (RS) K4, [p2, c6b, p2, k2] 4 times, k2.
Row 14: As Row 6. Rows 7 to 14 form cable and rib patt. Cont in patt,

Even if you've never cabled before, you'll find this wrap easy to make because the stitches are so large.

work 134 more rows, ending with a 12th patt row.
Next row: (RS) K4, [p2, slip next 3 sts onto cable needle, hold at back, k3, then work k2tog, k1 from cable needle, p2, k2] 4 times, k2. 50 sts. Patt 4 rows, ending with a RS row. Bind off knitwise.

TO FINISH
Weave in yarn ends.

ABOUT THIS YARN
Bigga is a soft, bulky yarn that knits up really quickly. It's a mix of 50% wool and 50% acrylic with approx. 44 yds. (40 m) to a 100 g (42 oz.) ball.

This dramatic, flattering wrap is in a soft ribbon yarn
that drapes to shape around your body beautifully.

Ribbon-yarn wrap

This is an easy lace pattern. There are just two rows, and the stitch count is the same on every row. On right-side rows, each pair of yarnover increases is compensated for by working three stitches together. Every wrong-side row is purl, apart from the knitted-edge stitches. Because the side edges are knitted in, there's almost no finishing—just weave in the yarn ends.

ESTIMATED TIME TO COMPLETE
The wrap took 26 hours to knit.

ABOUT THIS YARN
Sirdar Duet is a machine washable, 56% cotton and 44% nylon ribbon yarn with alternating matte and shiny areas, and it is available in pastel and natural shades, as well as black. There are 142 yds. (130 m) to a 50 g (approx. 1¾ oz.) ball.

SIZE
Width: 18 in. (46 cm); **length:** 72 in. (182 cm).

YOU WILL NEED
- 7 x 50 g balls (approx. 12½ oz.) of Sirdar Duet in Black, shade 745
- pair of size US 10 (6 mm) knitting needles

GAUGE
20 sts and 20 rows to 4 in. (10 cm) over patt on size US 10 (6 mm) needles. Change needle size, if necessary, to obtain this gauge.

ABBREVIATIONS
k = knit; **patt** = pattern; **p** = purl; **RS** = right side; **sk2po** = slip 1, k2tog, pass slipped st over; **st(s)** = stitch(es); **WS** = wrong side; **yo** = yarn to front and over needle to make a stitch; **[ ]** = work instructions in square brackets as directed.

NOTES
- Join in new yarn on the inner edge of the k4 edging. This will make it easier to hide the ends when darning them in.
- Cast on loosely so that the edge is flexible enough to wave as the stitch pattern is worked.

TIPS

- If you prefer to count in rows, you'll need to work 365 rows in pattern.

- As the wrap gets longer, roll up the lower edge and secure it with safety pins (taking care not to split the stitches when inserting them) to keep the end of the knitting out of the way and to stop it from catching on things and pulling threads.

WRAP
Cast on 91 sts. K 2 rows.
Work in patt, as follows:
Row 1 (RS) K4, [yo, k4, sk2po, k4, yo, k1] 7 times, k3.
Row 2 K4, p to last 4 sts, k4.

These 2 rows form the patt. Cont in patt until work, laid flat, measures nearly 72 in. (182 cm), ending with a RS row. K 2 rows.
Bind off knitwise.
Weave in yarn ends.

Striped afghan

Looks complicated, but it's easy, because you work with only one color at a time to make the cable panels, then sew them together to create the effect of stripes. Even if you've never done cables before, the yarn is so thick that you'll find it easy to work this bold braid.

ESTIMATED TIME TO COMPLETE
Each cable panel took 2½ hours; sewing them together and making the tassels took about 1½ hours: 9 hours total.

ABOUT THIS YARN
Rowan Big Wool is a thick, soft 100% merino wool yarn. There are 87 yds. (80 m) to a 100 g (approx. 3½ oz.) ball.

SIZE
Width: 17½ in. (44.5 cm); **length:** 55 in. (140 cm) (excluding tassels).

YOU WILL NEED
* 5 x 100 g (approx. 17½ oz.) balls of Rowan Big Wool in Ice Blue, shade 21 (A)
* 3 x 100 g (approx. 10½ oz.) balls same in Whoosh, shade 14 (B)
* pair of size US 17 (12 mm) knitting needles
* large cable needle

GAUGE
17 sts measure 6 in. (15 cm); 11 rows 4 in. (10 cm), over cable panel patt on size US 17 (12 mm) needles. Change needle size, if necessary, to obtain this gauge.

ABBREVIATIONS
c6b = slip next 3 sts onto cable needle and hold at back of work, k3, k3 from cable needle; **c6f** = slip next 3 sts onto cable needle and hold at front of work, k3, k3 from cable needle; **cont** = continue; **k** = knit; **patt** = pattern; **p** = purl; **RS** = right side; **st(s)** = stitch(es).

TIPS

● Each panel takes 2 balls of yarn. If you want a wrap without the tassels, you'll need one ball less in each color.

● If you want a wider wrap, make more panels, allowing two extra balls of yarn for each 6-in.- (15-cm)- wide panel.

● If you want a longer wrap, simply work longer panels. For example, one extra ball of A would allow you to make each of the 2 panels in A approximately 14 in. (35 cm) longer.

CABLE PANEL
Using A, cast on 19 sts.
Row 1 (RS) K3, p2, k9, p2, k3.
Row 2 P3, k2, p9, k2, p3.
Row 3 K3, p2, c6b, k3, p2, k3.
Rows 4, 5, and 6 Work Rows 2, 1, and 2 again.
Row 7 K3, p2, k3, c6f, p2, k3.
Row 8 As Row 2.
These 8 rows form cable panel patt. Patt 145 more rows, ending with a patt Row 1. Bind off knitwise.

Make one more cable panel in A and one in panel B.

TO FINISH
Placing B panel in the center, sew the panels together with mattress stitch (see page 154). Make 14 x 5-in. (12-cm) tassels, using 11 strands of yarn, 16 in. (40 cm) long, for each tassel. Sew 7 tassels on each end of the wrap.

Join boldly cabled strips to make this wonderful wrap.

Fluffy shrug

Cropped, curvy, and designed to fit closely, the body of this knit is just about as small as you can get, allowing the long sleeves to make the impact. It's all knitted in stockinette stitch, with simple shaping and no edgings.

ESTIMATED TIME TO COMPLETE
The shrug took around 27 hours to make, including sewing up.

ABOUT THIS YARN
Sirdar Gigi is a 100% nylon yarn with neon-bright contrasting knops of color twisted around a brushed core. It has approximately 126 yds. (115 m) to a 50 g (approx. 1¾ oz.) ball. Gigi makes a very soft fabric with a lot of drape. It should be hand-washed and dried flat, but there's no need to iron—just give it a shake and put it on.

SIZES
To fit: bust 30[**32**:34:**36**:38] in. (76[**81**:86:**91**:97] cm).
Actual measurements: back width 15¼[**16¼**:17¼:**18**:19] in. (39[**41.5**:44:**46**:48.5] cm); **length** 8½[**8¾**:9¼:**9½**:9¾] in. (22[**22.5**:23.5:**24.5**:25] cm); **sleeve** 18 in. (46 cm). Figures in square brackets refer to larger sizes; where there is one figure, it refers to all sizes.

YOU WILL NEED
• 6(**7**:7:**8**:8) x 50 g balls (approx. 10½[**12**:12:**14**:14] oz.) of Sirdar Gigi in black, shade 0046
• pair of size US 6 (4¼: mm) knitting needles

GAUGE
25 sts and 34 rows to 4 in. (10 cm) over st-st on size US 6 (4¼ mm) needles. Change needle size, if necessary, to obtain this gauge.

ABBREVIATIONS
beg = beginning; **cont** = continue; **dec** = decrease; **foll** = following; **inc** = increase; **k** = knit; **kfb** = k into front and back of st; **p** = purl; **RS** = right side; **skpo** = slip 1, k1, pass slipped st over; **st(s)** = stitch(es); **st-st** = stockinette st; **tog** = together; **WS** = wrong side.

NOTES
• To check your gauge, cast on 27 sts, and beg k row, st-st 36 rows. Place pins 1 stitch and 1 row in from each edge, and measure between pins. If you get less than 4 in. (10 cm), your knitting is too tight; try again, using larger needles. If you get more than 4 in. (10 cm), your knitting is too loose; try again, using smaller needles.
• Every row of the shaping for the front is written out.

TIPS

● Mark the increases with loops of smooth, contrasting yarn. This will make it easier to count the rows between shapings, and it will also help you to match the rows when sewing the sleeves together.

● The smooth side of stockinette stitch is given as the right side (RS) throughout, and the shrug in the picture is assembled in this way, but if you'd like a shrug with the knops of color showing less and the hairs on the surface showing more, assemble the shrug with the reverse, or purl (WS), side as the right side.

Knit this sweet little
mini-cardigan to wear
day or night.

A little bit of fluffiness makes for a glamorous evening shrug.

LEFT FRONT

Cast on 34(**37**:40:**43**:46) sts. Beg k row, st-st 2 rows.

Inc row (RS) K30(**33**:36:**39**:42), kfb, k3. Cont in st-st, inc in this way at front edge on next 5 RS rows. 40(**43**:46:**49**:52) sts. P 1 row.

Shape armhole. Row 1 (RS) Bind off 5(**6**:7:**8**:9) sts, k to last 4 sts, kfb, k3. P 1 row.

Row 3 K1, k2tog, k to last 4 sts, kfb, k3.

Cont in st-st, dec at beg and inc at end in same way as Row 3 on next 2 RS rows. 36(**38**:40:**42**:44) sts. Keeping front edge straight, dec at beg of next 4 RS rows. 32(**34**:36:**38**:40) sts. St-st 5 rows.

Shape neck. Dec row (RS) K to last 5 sts, skpo, k3. 31(**33**:35:**37**:39) sts. Cont in st-st, dec in this way at front edge on next 16(**17**:18:**19**:20) RS rows.15(**16**:17:**18**:19) sts. St-st 9(**9**:9:**11**:11) rows. Bind off.

RIGHT FRONT

Cast on 34(**37**:40:**43**:46) sts. Beg k row, st-st 2 rows.

Inc row (RS) K2, kfb, k to end. Cont in st-st, inc in this way at front edge on next 6 RS rows. 41(**44**:47:**50**:53) sts.

Shape armhole. Row 1 (WS) Bind off 5(**6**:7:**8**:9) sts, p to end.

Row 2 (RS) K2, kfb, k to last 3 sts, skpo, k1.

Cont in st-st, inc at beg and dec at end in same way as Row 3 on next 2 RS rows. 36(**38**:40:**42**:44) sts. Keeping front edge straight, dec at end of next 4 RS rows. 32(**34**:36:**38**:40) sts. St-st 5 rows.

Shape neck. Dec row (RS) K3, k2tog, k to end.

Cont in st-st, dec in this way at front edge on next 16(**17**:18:**19**:20) RS rows. 15(**16**:17:**18**:19) sts. St-st 9(**9**:9:**11**:11) rows. Bind off.

BACK

Cast on 98(**104**:110:**116**:122) sts. Beg k row, st-st 14 rows.

Shape armholes. Bind off 5(**6**:7:**8**:9) sts at beg of next 2 rows.

Dec row (RS) K1, k2tog, k to last 3 sts, skpo, k1.

Cont in st-st, dec in this way at each end of next 6 RS rows. 74(**78**:82:**86**:90) sts. St-st 39(**41**:43:**47**:49) rows.

Shape right side of neck.

Row 1 (RS) K24(**25**:26:**27**:28), turn and complete right side of shrug on these sts.

Row 2 Bind off 4 sts knitwise, p to end.

Row 3 K to last 2 sts, skpo.

Row 4 Bind off 3 sts knitwise, p to end.

Row 5 As Row 3. 15(**16**:17:**18**:19) sts.

St-st 3 rows. Bind off.

Shape left side of neck.

Row 1 (RS) Bind off center 26(**28**:30:**32**:34) sts purlwise, k to end. 24(**25**:26:**27**:28) sts.

Row 2 P to last 2 sts, p2tog.

Row 3 Bind off 4 sts purlwise, k to end.

Row 4 As Row 2.

Row 5 Bind off 3 sts purlwise, k to end. 15(**16**:17:**18**:19) sts.

St-st 3 rows. Bind off.

SLEEVES

Cast on 46(**48**:50:**52**:54) sts. Beg k row, st-st 20 rows.

Inc row (RS) K2, kfb, k to last 4 sts, kfb, k3.

Cont in st-st, inc in this way at each end of 16(**17**:18:**20**:21) foll 6th rows. 80(**84**:88:**94**:98) sts.

St-st until sleeve measures 18 in. (46 cm) from beg, ending with a p row.

Shape top. Bind off 5(**6**:7:**8**:9) sts at beg of next 2 rows.

Dec row (RS) K1, k2tog, k to last 3 sts, skpo, k1.

Cont in st-st, dec in this way at each end of next 6 RS rows. 56(**58**:60:**64**:66) sts.

St-st 3 rows.

Dec in same way as before at each end of next 4 RS rows. 48(**50**:52:**56**:58) sts.

P 1 row.

Next row (RS) Bind off 2 sts, k to last 2 sts, skpo.

Next row Bind off 2 sts, p to last 2 sts, p2tog.

Work last 2 rows 3 more times. 24(**26**:28:**32**:34) sts. Bind off.

TO FINISH

Join shoulder seams. Set in sleeves. Join side and sleeve seams. Weave in yarn ends.

Slouchy shrug

This knit is a flattering cross between a bolero and a shrug, so if you like the cropped-top look but want to cover up as well, it's ideal. The openwork-pattern rows are really easy: Simply wrap the yarn around the needle twice for each stitch; then, on the next row, drop the extra wraps to make long loops, which are crossed over. The other rows are just knit or purl.

ESTIMATED TIME TO COMPLETE
The first-size shrug took just 6 hours to make, including the edging.

ABOUT THIS YARN
Rowan Big Wool is a thick, soft, lightweight, 100% merino wool yarn. This colorway has two different shades twisted together. It has 87 yds. (80 m) to each 100 g (approx. 3½ oz.) ball and can be hand-washed or dry-cleaned.

SIZES
To fit: bust: 32 to 34[**36 to 38**:40 to 42] in. (81 to 86[**91 to 97**:101.5 to 107] cm)
Actual measurements: cuff to cuff 47[**49½**:52] in. (120[**126**:132] cm) with cuff folded back; **back length** 16¼[**18¼**:20¼] in. (41.5[**46.5**:51.5] cm) including edging. Figures in square brackets refer to larger sizes; where there is only one figure, it refers to all sizes.

YOU WILL NEED
• 4(**5**:6) x 100 g balls (approx. 14[**17½**:21] oz.) of Rowan Big Wool in Bohemian, shade 028
• pair each of size US 15 (10 mm) and size US 17 (12 mm) knitting needles
• 32-in. (81-cm)- long size US 17 (12 mm) circular needle

GAUGE
8 sts and 10 rows to 4 in. (10 cm) over crossed openwork patt on size US 17 (12 mm) needles. Change needle size, if necessary, to obtain this gauge.

ABBREVIATIONS
beg = beginning; **cont** = continue; **dec** = decrease; **foll** = following; **inc** = increase; **k** = knit; **kfb** = k into front and back of st; **patt** = pattern; **p** = purl; **RS** = right side; **skpo** = slip one, k1, pass slipped st over; **st(s)** = stitch(es); **st-st** = stockinette st; **tog** = together; **[ ]** = work instructions in square brackets as directed.

NOTES
• The shrug is knitted all in one piece, from cuff to cuff; then the edging is picked up and worked in the round.
• The increase and decrease rows for the sleeves are always on the 5th pattern row, which is a knit row.

SHRUG
Left sleeve. Using US 15 (10mm) needles, cast on 30(**34**:38) sts.
Row 1 (RS) K2, [p2, k2] to end.
Row 2 P2, [k2, p2] to end.
These 2 rows form rib patt. Rib 19 more rows.
Change to US 17 (12 mm) needles.
Row 1 (RS) P.
Row 2 Wrapping yarn twice around needle for each st, p all sts in row.
Row 3 Dropping the extra wraps for each st, k first st, [slip next 4 sts purlwise, return sts to left needle, k into front of 3rd st, lift over 2nd and first sts and off needle, k 4th st in same way, k first, then 2nd sts] 7(**8**:9) times, k1.
Row 4 K.
Row 5 K.
Row 6 P.
These 6 rows form crossed openwork patt.
Patt 10 more rows.
Inc row (RS) Kfb, k to last 2 sts, kfb, k1. 32(**36**:40) sts.
Cont in patt, crossing 2 sts at each end of patt Row 3 where necessary to keep patt correct, inc in this way at each end of 2 foll 6th rows. 36(**40**:44) sts.

Patt 5 rows.

Shape left armhole. Bind off 7 sts at beg of next 2 rows. 22(**26**:30) sts.

Back Patt 28(**34**:40) rows.

Shape armhole. Cast on 7 sts at beg of next 2 rows. 36(**40**:44) sts.

Right sleeve. Patt 4 rows.

Dec row (RS) K1, k2tog, k to last 3 sts, skpo, k1.

Cont in patt, dec in this way at each end of 2 foll 6th rows. 30(**34**:38) sts. Patt 17 rows.

Change to US 15 (10mm) needles.

Next row P2, [k2, p2] to end.

This row sets rib to match beg of left sleeve. Rib 20 more rows. Bind off in rib.

Edging. Join sleeve seams, reversing seam for turn-back cuff on ribbings. Using circular needle and beg at left sleeve seam, pick up 42(**46**:50) sts around lower edge of back to right sleeve seam and 42(**46**:50) sts around upper edge of back. 84(**92**:100) sts.

Round 1 P.

Round 2 [K1, p2, k1] to end. This round forms rib. Rib until edging measures 2¾ in. (7 cm). Bind off loosely in rib.

TIP

● If you don't have a size US 17 (12 mm) circular needle, use straight needles and work the edging in rows, in two pieces, before joining the sleeve seams. Just pick up half of the stated edging stitches at a time. Begin and end with k2 for the first rib row, then continue in rib as set for 2¾ in. (7 cm) and bind off. After completing the second side of the edging, join the sleeve and edging seams.

Softer than a shrug, bigger than a bolero, this natty knit can be slipped over a top for an added layer of style.

Summer shawl

This pretty lacy throw or shawl is made from garter-stitch squares and finished with a simple scalloped edging. Joining the decorative yarn-over increases around the squares is easy to do.

ESTIMATED TIME TO COMPLETE
The shawl took a total of 17 hours to make.

ABOUT THIS YARN
Debbie Bliss Merino DK is a 100% merino wool yarn and has 120 yds (110 m) to each 50g (approx. 1¾ oz.) ball.

SIZE
Width 24½ in. (62 cm); **length** 45 in. (114 cm).

YOU WILL NEED
- 7 x 50 g balls (approx. 12¼ oz.) of Debbie Bliss Merino DK in shade 615
- pair of size US 7 (4½ mm) knitting needles
- a spare size US 7 (4½ mm) needle
- size US 2 or C (2.5 mm) crochet hook

GAUGE
Each gst square measures 5 in. (13 cm), edging is 2 in. (5 cm) wide, both when pressed on size US 7 (4½ mm) needles. Change needle size, if necessary, to obtain these measurements.

ABBREVIATIONS
beg = beginning; **ch** = chain; **cont** = continue; **gst** = garter stitch; **inc** = increase; **k** = knit; **p** = purl; **RS** = right side; **st(s)** = stitch(es); **tog** = together; **WS** = wrong side; **yo** = yarn over needle to make a st; **yrh** = yarn around hook; **[ ]** = work instructions in square brackets as directed.

NOTE
- The needle size given is larger than usual for merino DK to add to the lightweight effect.

SHAWL
GARTER STITCH SQUARE
1st triangle Cast on one st.
Row 1 Yo, k1. 2 sts.
Row 2 Yo, k2. 3 sts.
Row 3 Yo, k3. 4 sts. Cont in gst, inc in this way at beg of every row until there are 26 sts. Cut yarn. Slip sts purlwise onto spare needle.

TIPS

● You can adapt this design to make any size shawl or afghan. Just plan the number of squares required and allow one more ball of yarn for each 6 squares extra you need to make, plus an extra ball for the edging if your afghan is really big.

● If you want to make larger or smaller gst squares, increase each triangle until you have a multiple of 3 sts plus 2. You can then join the triangles in the same way as given.

2nd triangle Work as given for 1st triangle but do not cut yarn.
Join triangles. Hold needles with triangles in left hand. Transfer yarn to left hand and cont with crochet hook. Insert hook knitwise into first st of each triangle and slip sts off needles, yrh and pull through, make 5ch. [Slip next 3 sts off front triangle onto hook, then slip next 3 sts off back triangle onto hook, yrh and pull through 6 sts, yrh and pull through 2 loops on hook, make 4ch] 8 times, insert hook in last st on each needle, yrh and pull through.
Make 32 squares.

EDGING
Cast on 7 sts.
Row 1 (RS) [Yo, p2tog] twice, k1, [yo] twice, k2.

Row 2 K2, dropping 2nd loop, work [k1, p1, k1] into double yo of previous row, k1, [yo, p2tog] twice.

Rows 3 and 5 [Yo, p2tog] twice, k6.

Row 4 K6, [yo, p2tog] twice.

Row 6 Bind off 3 sts loosely, one st on right needle, k2, [yo, p2tog] twice. 7 sts.

Work these 6 rows 109 more times. Bind off.

TO FINISH

Press squares pinning out decorative loops formed by the yarn over increases. Lay squares out in an oblong 4 squares wide by 8 squares long, making a pattern with the chain edge of the joins on WS as shown. Using lengths of yarn long enough to avoid joining in new yarn while sewing each seam, join first 8 pairs of blocks by oversewing the decorative loops together. Join squares for 2nd and 3rd long seams in the same way, then join the short seams. Placing cast-on edge in the center of one long side of the shawl and overlapping edging slightly, pin edging in place. Join cast-on and bound-off edges, then slip stitch edging in place.

Use this lightweight lacy knit as a shawl, a comforter, or an afghan.

Chevron poncho

The back and front of this poncho are knitted separately, then joined and worked in rounds, so there are no seams in the collar. The yarn is worked on larger needles than usual to make a light, flexible fabric.

Increases and decreases travel the stitches toward the center, creating a pointed edge that is emphasized by the chevron stripes that are made by the color changes in the yarn. The shaping is repetitive, so your fingers will soon learn exactly what to do and you will pick up speed after the first few rows.

You can make the second-size poncho, shown at lower right on page 71, in a week with just an hour of knitting each evening.

ESTIMATED TIME TO COMPLETE
The 2nd size poncho took 7 hours to make.

SIZES
To fit: bust 28 to 32[**34 to 38**:40 to 44] in. (71 to 81[**86 to 97**:101.5 to 112] cm)
Actual measurements: across shoulders 20¼[**22**:25] in. (51[**56**:63.5] cm);
around lower edge 55[**63**:71] in. (140[**160**:180] cm);
length at center front 13¾[**13¾**:16] in. (35[**35**:40.5] cm) excluding collar.
Figures in square brackets refer to larger sizes; where there is one figure, it refers to all sizes.

YOU WILL NEED
- 3(**4**:5) x 100 g hanks (approx. 10½[**14**:17½] oz.) of Noro Iro in shade 26
- pair of size US 11 (8 mm) knitting needles
- size US 10½ (7 mm) circular needle, 16 in. (40 cm) long

GAUGE
17 sts and 14 rows to 4 in. (10 cm) before pressing, 12 sts to 4 in. (10 cm) after pressing, over traveling rib, on size US 11 (8 mm) needles
Change needle size, if necessary, to obtain this gauge.

ABBREVIATIONS
beg = beginning; **cont** = continue; **dec** = decrease; **foll** = following; **k** = knit; **kfb** = k into front and back of st; **patt** = pattern; **p** = purl; **pfb** = p into front and back of st; **RS** = right side; **skpo** = slip 1, k1, pass slipped st over; **st(s)** = stitch(es); **tog** = together; **[ ]** = work instructions in square brackets as directed.

Ponchos have experienced a revival
and are now quite fashionable.

ABOUT THIS YARN
This 75% wool, 25% silk, bulky roving yarn has a hand-spun look. The color mix used here shades dramatically from soft black to hot pink, back to charcoal grey and finally to shades of green. One 100 g (approx. 3½ oz.) hank of Iro has about 131 yds. (120 m), (see page 159 for stockists).

PONCHO BACK
Cast on 86(**98**:110) sts.
Row 1 (RS) K2, [p4, k2] to end.
Row 2 P2, [k4, p2] to end.
Work in traveling rib.
Row 1 (RS) K1, [kfb, p3, k2tog] 7(**8**:9) times, [skpo, p2, pfb, k1] 7(**8**:9) times, k1.

Row 2 P2, [k4, p2] to end.
These 2 rows form traveling rib.
Work 28 more rows, ending with a
WS row.

Shape shoulders. Row 1 (RS) K1,
skpo, p2, k2tog, patt to last 7 sts,
skpo, p2, k2tog, k1. 82(**94**:106) sts.
Row 2 and every WS row rib as set.
Row 3 (RS) K1, skpo, k2tog, patt to
last 5 sts, skpo, k2tog, k1.
78(**90**:102) sts.

TIPS

● Mark the center rib as a reminder to
change from increasing and decreasing
to decreasing and increasing.

● Sew the seams with right sides
upward, using mattress stitch (see
page 154), taking 1 stitch in from each
edge so that the ribs match perfectly.

● If you want tassels for the fringed
edging, you'll need an extra ball of
yarn. Wrap yarn around a piece of
cardboard the depth of the fringe and
cut one edge. Use a crochet hook to
form tassels. Place one tassel at each
seam and at each point, and space
the remainder evenly.

Row 5 (RS) K1, skpo, kfb, patt
to last 4 sts, k1, k2tog, k1.
76(**88**:100) sts.
Row 7 (RS) K1, skpo, p3, k2tog, patt
to last 8 sts, skpo, p3, k2tog,
k1. 72(**84**:96) sts.
Row 9 (RS) K1, skpo, p1, k2tog, patt
to last 6 sts, skpo, p1, k2tog,
k1. 68(**80**:92) sts.
Row 11 (RS) K1, skpo, k1, patt to
last 4 sts, k1, k2tog, k1.
66(**78**:90) sts.
Row 13 (RS) K1, skpo, patt to last 3
sts, k2tog, k1. 64(**76**:88) sts.
Row 15 (RS) As Row 7.
60(**72**:84) sts.
3rd size only. Rows 17–23 Work as
given for Rows 9, 11, 13, and 7.

All sizes 60(**72**:72) sts.
Rib 1 row. Leave sts on a holder.

FRONT
Work as given for back.

TO FINISH
Join side seams.
Collar. Using circular needle, across
back neck sts work, * k2 tog, p2,
[k2tog, skpo, p2] to last 2 sts, skpo,
rep from * across front neck sts.
80(**96**:96) sts.
Round 1 [K1, p2, k1] to end.
This round forms rib. Rib until collar
measures 10¼in. (26 cm). Bind off.
Fold collar down. Weave in yarn ends.
Press lower edge of poncho only.

Jackets and tops

Now we're down to the real knitting—to more ambitious-looking garments. Yet although all of these projects require some shaping, each one has a trick that makes it easier than it looks. These garments are designed to enhance the inherent characteristics of the yarns. Enjoy their tactile qualities—from the sophistication of a smooth cashmere mix, which makes the ruffled edges of the wrap jacket flute so beautifully, to the subtle textures of bouclé or hand-spun-effect yarns to the shaggy chic of strips of ripped fabric. To speed up your work, many of these designs have easy, yet chic, edgings. One sweater is worked in the round from the top down, so there's almost no finishing necessary. Sleeveless designs, such as vests, yield even quicker results. And if you choose a big-yarn-and-big-needles project, you'll be wearing it in next to no time.

- ■ Loop-edge jacket
- ■ Ripped-fabric top
- ■ Fun-fur vest
- ■ Wrap jacket
- ■ Sparkle vest
- ■ Sheepskin-look vest
- ■ Dip-and-rip vest
- ■ Shaded jacket
- ■ Circular sweater
- ■ Blanket jacket

A decorative loopy edging adds
excitement to this very simple
fitted jacket.

Loop-edge jacket

A decorative loopy edging adds excitement to this very simple fitted jacket, knitted in a lightweight, but chunky, yarn.

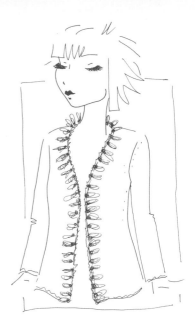

ESTIMATED TIME TO COMPLETE
Including finishing and working the loop-stitch edging, the 1st size jacket took 15 hours to make.

SIZES
To fit bust 32 to 34[**36 to 38**:40 to 42:**44 to 46**] in. (81 to 86[**91 to 97**: 101.5 to 107:**112 to 117**] cm).
Actual measurements: bust 39¼[**43¼**:48¼:**53**] in. (100[**110**:123:**135**] cm); **length** 24¼[**25**:26:**27**] in. (62[**63.5**:66:**68.5**] cm); **sleeve** 16½[**18**:18:**19**] in. (42[**46**:46:**48.5**] cm). Figures in square brackets refer to larger sizes; where there is one figure, it refers to all sizes.

YOU WILL NEED
- 9(**10**:11:**12**) x 100 g balls (approx. 31½[**35**:38½:**42**] oz.) of Sirdar Bigga in Blue Horizon, shade 673
- pair of size US 19 (15 mm) knitting needles
- size US 17 (12 mm) circular needle

GAUGE
6 sts and 9 rows to 4 in. (10 cm) over st-st on size US 19 (15 mm) needles. Change needle size, if necessary, to obtain this gauge.

ABBREVIATIONS
beg = beginning; **cont** = continue; **dec** = decrease; **foll** = following; **inc** = increase; **k** = knit; **kfb** = k into front and back of st; **p** = purl; **RS** = right side; **skpo** = slip one, k1, pass slipped st over; **st(s)** = stitch(es); **st-st** = stockinette st; **tog** = together; **WS** = wrong side.

NOTES
- Do not join in yarn at front edges.
- The circular needle is used to work back and forth in the usual way.

TIPS
● If you don't have a circular needle, use straight size 17 (12 mm) needles and pick up and work the loop-stitch edging in three sections: right front, back neck, and left front. Join the sections at the shoulders.

● Even if you've never picked up stitches before, you'll find it easy to see where to place the needle to hook the stitch through because of the knit stitch at the front edges. Simply go between the knit stitch and the first stitch in stockinette stitch. To pick up the stitches evenly on each front, skip approximately every 8th row end.

● When shaping the sleeve top, you'll get a smoother line if you slip the first stitch each time you bind off stitches.

JACKET
BACK
Using size US 19 (15 mm) needles, cast on 30(**33**:36:**39**) sts. Beg k row, st-st 4 rows.
Dec row (RS) K3, k2tog, k to last 5 sts, skpo, k3.
Cont in st-st, dec in this way at each end of 2 foll 6th rows. 24(**27**:30:**33**) sts. St-st 5 rows.
Inc row (RS) K2, kfb, k to last 4 sts, kfb, k3.
Cont in st-st, inc in this way at each end of 2 foll 4th rows. 30(**33**:36:**39**) sts. St-st 7 rows.
Shape armholes. Bind off 2 sts at beg of next 2 rows.
Dec row (RS) K1, k2tog, k to last 3 sts, skpo, k1.
Cont in st-st, dec in this way at each end of next 1(**1**:2:**2**) RS rows. 22(**25**:26:**27**) sts. St-st 13(**15**:15:17) rows.
Bind off purlwise.

RIGHT FRONT

Using size US 19 (15 mm) needles, cast on 15(**17**:19:**21**) sts.

Row 1 (RS) K.

Row 2 P to last st, k1.

These 2 rows form st-st with k1 at front edge. Work 2 more rows.

Dec row (RS) K to last 5 sts, skpo, k3. 14(**16**:18:**20**) sts.

Dec in this way at end of 2 foll 6th rows. 12(**14**:16:**18**) sts.

Work 5 rows.

Inc row (RS) K to last 4 sts, kfb, k3. 13(**15**:17:**19**) sts.

Inc in this way at end of 2 foll 4th rows. 15(**17**:19:**21**) sts.

Work 8 rows, ending with a RS row.

Shape armhole and neck. Bind off 2 sts at beg of next row.

Dec row (RS) K2, k2tog, k to last 3 sts, skpo, k1.

Dec in this way at each end of next 1(**1**:2:**2**) RS rows.

9(**11**:11:**13**) sts.

Dec at neck edge only on foll 4(**5**:4:**5**) RS rows. 5(**6**:7:**8**) sts.

Work 5(**5**:7:**7**) rows. Bind off.

SLEEVES

Using size US 19 (15 mm) needles, cast on 16(**17**:18:**19**) sts. Beg k row, st-st 4(**4**:4:**2**) rows.

Inc row (RS) K2, kfb, k to last 4 sts, kfb, k3. 18(**19**:20:21) sts.

Cont in st-st, inc in this way at each end of 3(**4**:4:**5**) foll 8th rows. 24(**27**:28:**31**) sts. St-st 9(**5**:5:**1**) rows.

Shape top. Bind off 2 sts at beg of next 2 rows.

Dec row (RS) K1, k2tog, k to last 3 sts, skpo, k1.

Cont in st-st, dec in this way at each end of next 4 RS rows.

10(**13**:14:**17**) sts.

P 1 row.

LEFT FRONT

Using size US 19 (15 mm) needles, cast on 15(**17**:19:**21**) sts.

Row 1 (RS) K.

Row 2 K1, p to end.

These 2 rows form st-st with k1 at front edge. Work 2 more rows.

Dec row (RS) K3, k2tog, k to end.

Cont in st-st, dec in this way at beg of 2 foll 6th rows. 12(**14**:16:**18**) sts. St-st 5 rows.

Inc row (RS) K2, kfb, k to end.

Cont in st-st, inc in this way at beg of 2 foll 4th rows. 15(**17**:19:**21**) sts.

Work 7 rows.

Shape armhole and neck. Bind off 2 sts at beg of next row. 13(**15**:17:**19**) sts.

P 1 row.

Dec row (RS) K1, k2tog, k to last 4 sts, skpo, k2.

Dec in this way at each end of next 1(**1**:2:**2**) RS rows. 9(**11**:11:**13**) sts.

Dec at neck edge only on foll 4(**5**:4:**5**) RS rows.

5(**6**:7:**8**) sts.

Work 5(**5**:7:**7**) rows.

Bind off.

Next row (RS) Bind off 2 sts, k to last 2 sts, skpo.

Next row Bind off 2 sts, p to last 2 sts, p2tog. 4(**7**:8:**11**) sts. Bind off.

EDGING

Matching sts, join shoulders. Using circular needle, pick up 49(**50**:52:**53**) sts up right front to shoulder, 12 sts across back neck, and 49(**50**:52:**53**) sts down left front to lower edge. 110(**112**:116:**118**) sts. K 1 row.

Next row (RS) K into front of first st but leave st on left needle, bring yarn forward between needles; take it around left thumb and back between needles, leaving a loop of yarn held by thumb on RS; k into back of first st and allow st to drop off left needle; remove thumb from loop, lift first st over 2nd st and off right needle; k each st in this way to end.
Bind off knitwise.

TO FINISH

Set in sleeves. Taking a half stitch from each side, join side and sleeve seams.

ABOUT THIS YARN

Bigga is a super-thick 50% wool, 50% acrylic yarn that's surprisingly light-weight. It has approx. 44 yds. (40 m) to a 100 g ball (approx. 3½ oz.).

This loop-edged jacket is a perfect topper for your favorite pair of jeans.

Ripped-fabric top

Choose lightweight cotton in solid colors, prints, or color-woven stripes to create the "yarn." (All that ripping is really good for releasing tension!) Knotting the strips gives added texture to the garter stitch used to make this simple slip-on-and-tie top.

ESTIMATED TIME TO COMPLETE
It took 1½ hours to rip, knot, and wind the balls of "yarn," then just 3 hours to knit the top: 4½ hours total.

ABOUT THIS YARN
Use 100% cotton fabrics in different colors to make the "yarn." The top in the photo at right used about 6 or 7 different stripe patterns and four contrasting solid colors. For a really multi-colored effect, rip the strips, then mix up the colors before knotting the strips together.

SIZES
To fit bust 32[**34**:36:**38**] in. (81[**86**:91:**97**] cm).
Actual measurements: bust 31½[**33½**:36:**38**] in. (80[**85.5**:91:**97**] cm); **length** 15[**16½**:17¾:**19¼**] in. (38[**42**:45:**49**] cm). Figures in square brackets refer to larger sizes; where there is only one figure, it refers to all sizes.

YOU WILL NEED
• 10(**11**:12:**13**) pieces of cotton fabric, approximately 20 x 22 in. (51 x 56 cm), each ripped lengthwise into 25 strips, ¾ in. (2 cm) wide, and knotted together to make a total length of approximately 122[**134**:147:**159**] yds. (112.5[**123**:135:**146**] m) of yarn
• sharp scissors
• pair of size US 35 (20 mm) knitting needles

GAUGE
7 sts and 5½ rows to 4 in. (10 cm) over gst on size US 35 (20 mm) needles. Change needle size, if necessary, to obtain this gauge.

ABBREVIATIONS
beg = beginning; **cont** = continue; **gst** = garter st; **k** = knit; **RS** = right side; **skpo** = slip 1, k1, pass slipped st over, **st(s)** = stitch(es); **tog** = together.

NOTES
• To make the strips, first snip the raw edge of the fabric, then rip.
• The side seams should be joined edge to edge.

Rip up cotton fabric and knot the strips to make a colorful "yarn" for knitting this quick tie-front top.

These fabric strip "yarns" are so much fun to make and knit, you may find yourself wanting to make several of these colorful vests.

BACK

Cast on 28(**30**:32:**34**) sts. K 10 rows.

Shape armholes. Bind off 2 sts at beg of next 2 rows. 24(**26**:28:**30**) sts.

Dec row (RS) K2tog, k to last 2 sts, skpo. 22(**24**:26:**28**) sts.

Cont in gst, dec in this way at each end of next 2 RS rows. 18(**20**:22:**24**) sts. K 4(**6**:8:**10**) rows, ending with a RS row. Bind off.

LEFT FRONT

Cast on 14(**15**:16:**17**) sts. K 10 rows **.

Shape neck and armhole.

Row 1 (RS) Bind off 2 sts, k to last 2 sts, skpo. 11(**12**:13:**14**) sts. K 1 row. Cont in gst, dec one st at each end of next row and foll RS row, then dec at end of next 3 RS rows. 4(**5**:6:**7**) sts. K 0(**2**:4:**6**) rows. Bind off.

RIGHT FRONT

Work as given for left front to **.

Shape neck and armhole.

Row 1 (RS) K2tog, k to end.

Row 2 Bind off 2 sts, k to end. 11(**12**:13:**14**) sts.

Cont in gst, dec one st at each end of next row and foll RS row, then dec at beg of next 3 RS rows. 4(**5**:6:**7**) sts. K 0(**2**:4:**6**) rows. Bind off.

TO FINISH

Join shoulder and side seams. Thread a strip of fabric through fronts and tie as shown above.

TIPS

● Check out patchwork cotton fabrics sold in "fat quarters" for a variety of good, strong colors and patterns.

● If you want to recycle fabric from old garments, such as skirts or shirts, make sure that they are 100% cotton, because polyester or nylon won't rip easily or create nicely frayed edges.

Fun-fur vest

This yarn makes such a densely textured surface that there's no need to bother with edgings and changing needle sizes; just cast on and go, to create a super furry fabric. The vest is knitted entirely in stockinette stitch. Three simple pieces form the back and fronts, which are slightly shaped to follow the body line; for the collar, just pick up neckline stitches and work straight.

ESTIMATED TIME TO COMPLETE
The back and fronts took around 18 hours; making the collar and sewing the seams took another 3 hours. The vest took 21 hours in total.

ABOUT THIS YARN
Sirdar Funky Fur is a 100% polyester yarn with a twisted core that has long, fine threads springing out to create a furry surface. It is machine washable and has approximately 98 yds. (90 m) to a 50 g (approx. 1¾ oz.) ball.

SIZES
To fit bust 32[**34**:36:**38**] in. (81[**86**:91:**97**] cm)
Actual measurements: bust 35½[**37¾**:40:**42**] in. (90.5[**96**:101.5:**107**] cm); length 19¾[**20**:21:**21½**] in. (50[**51**:53.5:**55**] cm). Figures in square brackets refer to larger sizes; where there is one figure, it refers to all sizes.

YOU WILL NEED
• 8(**9**:10:**11**) x 50 g balls (approx. 14[**15¾**:17½:**19¼**] oz.) of Sirdar Funky Fur in Inky Blue, shade 0530
• pair of size US 6 (4¼ mm) knitting needles

GAUGE
22 sts and 32 rows to 4 in. (10 cm) over st-st on size US 6 (4¼ mm) needles. Change needle size, if necessary, to obtain this gauge.

ABBREVIATIONS
beg = beginning; **cont** = continue; **dec** = decrease; **foll** = following; **inc** = increase; **k** = knit; **kfb** = k into front and back of st; **p** = purl; **RS** = right side; **skp**o = slip 1, k1, pass slipped st over; **st(s)** = stitch(es); **st-st** = stockinette st; **tog** = together.

NOTE
• Mark the ends of the increase rows with a loop of smooth, contrasting yarn. This will make it easier to see how many increases have been worked; and if you leave the loops in, it will help you match rows when sewing the vest together.

BACK
Cast on 90(**96**:102:**108**) sts.
Beg k row, work in st-st until back measures 4¼ in. (11 cm), ending with a p row.
Inc row (RS) K1, kfb, k to last 3 sts, kfb, k2.
Cont in st-st in this way at each end of 4 foll 8th rows.
100(**106**:112:**118**) sts.
St-st until back measures 12[**12**:12¾:**12¾**] in. (30.5[**30.5**:32.5:**32.5**] cm) from beg, ending with a p row.
Shape armholes. Bind off 5(**6**:7:**8**) sts at beg of next 2 rows.
Dec row (RS) K1, k2tog, k to last 3 sts, skpo, k1. 88(**92**:96:**100**) sts.
Cont in st-st, dec in this way at each end of next 6 RS rows.
76(**80**:84:**88**) sts. St-st until back measures 19¾[**20**:21:**21½**] in. (50.5[**51**:53.5:**55**] cm) from beg, ending with a p row.
Bind off.

You'll have all the fun of the fur and none of the guilt with this lightweight slip-on vest.

This fun-fur yarn
is versatile; use
it for making
skinny scarves,
as well as this
easy vest.

LEFT FRONT

Cast on 45(**48**:51:**54**) sts.

Beg k row, st-st until front measures 4¼ in. (11 cm), ending with a p row **.

Inc row (RS) K1, kfb, k to end.

Cont in st-st, inc in this way at beg of 4 foll 8th rows. 50(**53**:56:**59**) sts. St-st until front measures 12[**12**:12¾:**12¾**] in. (30.5[**30.5**:32.5:**32.5**] cm) from beg, ending with a p row.

Shape armhole. Bind off 5(**6**:7:**8**) sts at beg of next row. P 1 row.

Dec row (RS) K1, k2tog, k to end.

Cont in st-st, dec in this way at beg of next 6 RS rows. 38(**40**:42:**44**) sts. St-st until front measures 17½[**17¾**:18¾:**19¼**] in. (44.5[**45**:47.5:**49**] cm) from beg, ending with a k row.

Shape neck. Bind off 11(**12**:13:**14**) sts at beg of next row.

Dec row (RS) K to last 2 sts, skpo.

Cont in st-st, dec in this way at end of next 7 RS rows. 19(**20**:21:**22**) sts. Work 3 rows straight. Bind off.

RIGHT FRONT

As left front to **.

Inc row (RS) K to last 3 sts, kfb, k2.

Cont in st-st, inc in this way at end of 4 foll 8th rows. 50(**53**:56:**59**) sts. St-st until front measures 12[**12**:12¾:**12¾**] in. (30.5[**30.5**:32.5:**32.5**] cm) from beg, ending with a k row.

Shape armhole. Bind off 5(**6**:7:**8**) sts at beg of next row.

Dec row (RS) K to last 3 sts, skpo, k1.

Cont in st-st, dec in this way at end of next 6 RS rows. 38(**40**:42:**44**) sts. St-st until front measures 17½[**17¾**:18¾:**19¼**] in. (44.5[**45**:47.5:**49**] cm) from beg, ending with a p row.

Shape neck. Bind off 11(**12**:13:**14**) sts at beg of next row. P 1 row.

Dec row (RS) K2tog, k to end. Cont in st-st, dec in this way at beg of next 7 RS rows. 19(**20**:21:**22**) sts. St-st 3 rows straight. Bind off.

COLLAR

Matching sts, join shoulder seams. With RS facing, pick up and k 26(**27**:28:**29**) sts up right front neck, 36(**38**:40:**42**) sts across back neck and 26(**27**:28:**29**) sts down left front neck. 88(**92**:96:**100**) sts. Beg with a p row, st-st until collar measures 6¼ in. (16 cm), ending with a k row. Bind off.

TO FINISH

Join side seams. Weave in yarn ends.

This stylish jacket is gently shaped at the sides to give a flattering fit and has high armholes with slim sleeves that flare over the wrists.

Wrap jacket

Although it's knitted entirely in simple stockinette stitch, this jacket is constructed in an unusual way. The back and sleeves are knitted conventionally, but the fronts are knitted sideways, so the ruffle "grows" out from the front edges.

ESTIMATED TIME TO COMPLETE
The first size jacket took a total of 27 hours, including finishing.

ABOUT THIS YARN
Debbie Bliss Cashmerino Aran is a supple, lightweight yarn that's a mix of 55% merino wool, 33% microfiber, and 12% cashmere. It has approximately 99 yds. (90 m) to a 50 g (approx. 1¾ oz.) ball.

SIZES
To fit: bust 34 to 36[**38** to **40**:42 to 44:**46** to **48**] in. (86 to 91[**97** to **101.5**:107 to 112:**117** to **122**] cm)
Actual measurements: bust 38[**42¼**:46½:**51**] in. (97[**107**:118:**129.5**] cm) excluding wrap-over; l**ength** 23[**23¾**:24½:**25**] in. (58.5[**60.5**:62:**63.5**] cm); **sleeve** 18¾ in. (47.5 cm). Figures in square brackets refer to larger sizes; where there is one figure, it refers to all sizes.

YOU WILL NEED
- 13(**15**:17:**19**) x 50 g balls (approx. 22¾[**26¼**:29¾:**33¼**] oz.) of Debbie Bliss Cashmerino Aran in shade 502
- pair of size US 8 (5 mm) knitting needles
- 39-in. (99-cm) long size US 8 (5 mm) circular needle
- pin or brooch (optional)

GAUGE
18 sts and 24 rows to 4 in. (10 cm) over st-st on size US 8 (5mm) needles. Change needle size, if necessary, to obtain this gauge.

ABBREVIATIONS
beg = beginning; **cont** = continue; **dec** = decrease; **foll** = following; **inc** = increase; **k** = knit; **kfb** = k into front and back of st; **p** = purl; **RS** = right side; **skpo** = slip 1, k1, pass slipped st over; **sl** = slip; **st(s)** = stitch(es); **st-st** = stockinette st; **tog** = together; **WS** = wrong side; **yb** = yarn to back of work; **yf** = yarn to front of work; **[ ]** = work instructions in square brackets as directed.

TIPS

● To create a smoother line when binding off the groups of 2 stitches to shape the back neck and top of the sleeves, slip the first stitch.

● When sewing the shoulders and side seams, you will need to join approximately 9 stitches to every 12 rows.

● Always sew with the right side of the garment facing you; it's easier to join stitches and rows this way, and to match the sleeve shapings.

● Pin the seams at regular intervals before joining, to make sure that they don't slip as you sew. Use either blunt-pointed knitter's pins or large glass-headed pins, and insert them at right angles to the seam; this way, they won't work loose.

● If you don't have a circular needle, you can use 2 pairs of straight needles to hold the stitches for the ruffle. Simply knit until the first needle is nearly full, then continue with the second, then the third needle.
Use the fourth to knit with. Take care not to leave loose stitches when changing needles.

BACK

Cast on 87(**97**:107:**117**) sts. Beg k row, st-st 16 rows.

Dec row (RS) K2, k2tog, k to last 4 sts, skpo, k2. 85(**95**:105:**115**) sts.

Cont in st-st, dec in this way at each end of 3 foll 8th rows.

79(**89**:99:**109**) sts.

St-st 9 rows.

Inc row (RS) K1, kfb, k to last 3 sts, kfb, k2. 81(**91**:101:**111**) sts.

Cont in st-st, inc in this way at each end of 3 foll 8th rows.

87(**97**:107:**117**) sts.

St-st 17 rows.

Shape armholes. Bind off 4(**5**:6:**7**) sts at beg of next 2 rows.

79(**87**:95:**103**) sts.

Dec in same way as before at each end of next 6(**7**:8:**9**) RS rows.

67(**73**:79:**85**) sts.

St-st 31(**33**:35:**37**) rows.

Shape neck. Next row (RS) K22(**24**:26:**28**), turn and complete right-hand side on these sts. [Bind off 2 sts at beg of next row and dec 1 st at end of foll row] twice.

16(**18**:20:**22**) sts. P 1 row. Bind off. With RS facing, bind off center 23(**25**:27:**29**) sts, k to end.

22(**24**:26:**28**) sts.

[Dec 1 st at end of next row and bind off 2 sts at beg of foll row] twice.

16(**18**:20:**22**) sts. P 1 row. Bind off.

RIGHT FRONT

Cast on 68 sts.

Shape side and armhole.

Row 1 (RS) K.

Row 2 P33, sl 1, yb, turn and leave 34 sts.

Row 3 Sl 1, yb, k33.

Row 4 P26, sl 1, yb, turn and leave 7 more sts.

Row 5 Sl 1, yb, k24, kfb, k1.

Row 6 P20, sl 1, yb, turn and leave 7 more sts.

Row 7 Sl 1, yb, k18, kfb, k1.

Row 8 P. 70 sts.

Row 9 K to last 2 sts, kfb, k1. 71 sts. Work Rows 8 and 9 0(**1**:2:**3**) more times, then work Row 8 again.

71(**72**:73:**74**) sts.

Next row K to last 2 sts, kfb, k1, cast on 34(**37**:39:**41**) sts.

106(**110**:113:**116**) sts.

Shoulder. St-st 20(**24**:26:**30**) rows, ending with a k row.

Shape neck. Next row (WS) Bind off 8(**9**:10:**11**) sts, p to end.

98(**101**:103:**105**) sts.

Dec row (RS) K to last 3 sts, skpo, k1. 97(**100**:102:**104**) sts.

Cont in st-st, dec in this way at end of next 22(**23**:24:**25**) RS rows.

75(**77**:78:**79**) sts.

St-st 2 rows. Leave sts on a holder.

LEFT FRONT

Cast on 68 sts.

Shape side and armhole.

Row 1 (RS) K.

Row 2 P.

Row 3 K33, yf, sl 1, yb, turn and leave 34 sts.

Row 4 Sl 1, p33.

Row 5 Kfb, k25, yf, sl 1, yb, turn and leave 7 more sts.

Row 6 Sl 1, p 27.

Row 7 Kfb, k19, yf, sl 1, yb, turn and leave 7 more sts.

Row 8 Sl 1, p21.

Row 9 Kfb, k to end. 71 sts.

Row 10 P.

Work Rows 9 and 10 0(**1**:2:**3**) more times, then work Row 9 again. 72(**73**:74:**75**) sts.

Next row P72(**73**:74:**75**), cast on 34(**37**:39:**41**) sts. 106(**110**:113:**116**) sts.

Shoulder. St-st 20(**24**:26:**30**) rows, ending with a p row.

Shape neck. Next row (RS) Bind off 8(**9**:10:**11**) sts, 1 st on right needle, k2tog, k to end. 97(**100**:102:**104**) sts. P 1 row.

Dec row (RS) K1, k2tog, k to end. 96(**99**:101:**103**) sts.

Cont in st-st, dec in this way at beg of next 21(**22**:23:**24**) RS rows. 75(**77**:78:**79**)sts.

P 1 row. Leave sts on a holder.

SLEEVES

Cast on 57(**63**:69:**75**) sts.

Beg k row, st-st 12 rows.

Dec row (RS) K2, [k2tog, k1, skpo, k1] 9(**10**:11:**12**) times, k1. 39(**43**:47:**51**) sts.

St-st 7(**3**:7:**7**) rows.

Inc row (RS) K1, kfb, k to last 3 sts, kfb, k2. 41(**45**:49:**53**) sts.

Cont in st-st, inc in this way at each end of 11(**12**:13:**14**) foll 8th(**8th**:6th: **6th**) rows. 63(**69**:75:**81**) sts.

St-st 5(**1**:15:**9**) rows.

Shape top. Bind off 4(**5**:6:**7**) sts at beg of next 2 rows. 55(**59**:63:**67**) sts.

Dec row K1, k2tog, k to last 3 sts, skpo, k1. 53(**57**:61:**65**) sts.

Cont in st-st, dec in this way at each end of next 5(**6**:7:**8**) RS rows. 43(**45**:47:**49**) sts.

St-st 7 rows.

Dec as before at each end of next 4 RS rows. 35(**37**:39:**41**) sts.

P1 row.

Next row (RS) Bind off 2 sts, k to last 2 sts, skpo. 32(**34**:36:**38**) sts.

Next row Bind off 2 sts, p to last 2 sts, p2tog. 29(**31**:33:**35**) sts.

Work last 2 rows 3 more times. 11(**13**:15:**17**) sts. Bind off.

RUFFLE

Join shoulders. Using circular needle, slip 75(**77**:78:**79**) sts from right front holder, pick up and k 39(**43**:47:**50**) sts up right front neck, 39(**42**:42:**44**) sts around back neck, and 39(**43**:47:**50**) sts down left front neck, k 75(**77**:78:**79**) sts from left front holder. 267(**282**:292:**302**) sts.

Row 1 and every WS row P.

Row 2 Kfb, [k4, kfb] 53(**56**:58:**60**) times, k1. 321(**339**:351:**363**) sts.

Row 4 Kfb, [kfb, k4, kfb] 53(**56**:58:**60**) times, kfb, k1. 429(**453**:469:**485**) sts.

Row 6 Kfb, [k2, kfb, k4, kfb] 53(**56**:58:**60**) times, k2, kfb, k1. 537(**567**:587:**607**) sts.

Row 8 K.

Row 10 Kfb, [k4, kfb] 107(**113**:117:**121**) times, k1. 645(**681**:705:**729**) sts.

Row 12 K.

Row 14 Kfb, [k6, kfb,k4, kfb] 53(**56**:58:**60**) times, k6, kfb, k1. 753(**795**:823:**851**) sts.

Row 16 K.

Row 18 K.

Bind off knitwise.

TO FINISH

Press according to yarn label. Set in sleeves. Join side and sleeve seams. Weave in yarn ends.

Sparkle vest

Fine yarn knits up quickly in a fascinating stitch pattern on large needles. Just straight knitting with a little shaping for the front makes this simple little top. Sew on sequins and beads for extra sparkle.

ESTIMATED TIME TO COMPLETE
The 2nd size vest took 14 hours to make.

SIZE
Stretches to fit: bust 32[**34**:36:**38**] in. (81[**86**:91:**97**] cm).
Actual measurements: bust 30¼[**31½**:33¼:**34½**] in. (77[**80**:84.5:**88**] cm); **length** to center front 14¼[**15**:16:**16¾**] in. (36[**38**:40.5:**42.5**] cm). Figures in square brackets refer to larger sizes; where there is one figure, it refers to all sizes.

YOU WILL NEED
* 4(**4**:5:**5**) x 25 g balls (approx 3½[**3½**:4½:**4½** oz.]) of Rowan Lurex Shimmer in Minty, shade 337
* pair each of size US 3 (3¼ mm) and size US 10 (6 mm) knitting needles
* assorted sequins and beads
* matching sewing thread and a fine, sharp needle

GAUGE
22 sts and 20 rows to 4 in. (10 cm) over daisy patt on size US 10 (6 mm) needles. Change needle size, if necessary, to obtain this gauge.

ABBREVIATIONS
beg = beginning; **cont** = continue; **dec** = decrease; **k** = knit; **patt** = pattern; **p** = purl; **p3yo3** = p3tog but leave sts on left needle, yarn around needle, p same 3 sts tog and slip sts off left needle; **RS** = right side; **s2kpo** = slip next 2 sts as if to k2tog, k1, pass 2 slipped sts over; **st(s)** = stitch(es); **st-st** = stockinette stitch; **WS** = wrong side; **[ ]** = work instructions in square brackets as directed.

NOTES
* The daisy-stitch pattern starts in a different place on the back and the front so the pattern matches at the side seams.
* Work the yo of the p3yo3 quite loosely, so it's easy to knit into it on the next row.
* Working double decreases for the armhole shaping takes off 2 sts at each end and keeps the pattern correct.
* The openwork stitch pattern is very stretchy, so the top will shape itself to the body.
* Although Lurex Shimmer can be pressed, do not press the completed top as this will flatten the stitch pattern.

TIPS

● The pattern row for this pretty openwork stitch is easier to work if you tuck the end of the right needle under your arm, leaving your right hand free to wrap the yarn for the p3yo3.

● Because you're making 3 stitches each time you take 3 stitches together, the stitch count is the same on every row. Once you've completed a few repeats, it becomes easy to see how the grouped stitches alternate, making it easy to work the stitch pattern without constantly referring to the instructions.

● Before binding off the first strap, try the top on and, if necessary, adjust the length of the strap.

● Sewing on antique beads or beads from a broken necklace would add to the vintage effect.

● Never press sequins; they will curl.

VEST

BACK

Using size US 3 (3¼ mm) needles, cast on 85(**89**:93:**97**) sts.

Row 1 (RS) K.

Row 2 P1, [yo, p2tog] to end.

Row 3 K.

Row 4 K.

These 4 rows form the edging **. Change to size US 10 (6 mm) needles.

Row 1 (RS) K.

Row 2 K1, p1, k1, [p3yo3, k1] to last 2 sts, p1, k1.

Row 3 K.

Row 4 K1, [p3yo3, k1] to end.

These 4 rows form daisy patt. Work 54(**58**:62:**66**) more rows, ending with a 2nd patt row.

Using US 3 (3¼ mm) needles, bind off knitwise.

FRONT

Work as given for back to **. Change to US 10 (6 mm) needles.

Row 1 (RS) K.

Row 2 K1, [p3yo3, k1] to end.

Row 3 K.

Row 4 K1, p1, k1, [p3yo3, k1] to last 2 sts, p1, k1.

These 4 rows form daisy patt. Work 54(**58**:62:**66**) more rows, ending with a 2nd patt row.

Shape armholes. Row 1 (RS) Bind off 2 sts, k to end. 83(**87**:91:**95**) sts.

Row 2 Bind off 2 sts, 1 st on right needle, [p3yo3, k1] to end. 81(**85**:89:**93**) sts.

Row 3 (RS) S2kpo, k to last 3 sts, s2kpo. 77(**81**:85:**89**) sts.

Row 4 K1, [p3yo3, k1] to end.

Cont in patt, dec in same way as Row 3 at each end of next 5 RS rows. 57(**61**:65:**69**) sts.

Using size US 3 (3¼ mm) needles, bind off knitwise.

If you prefer, sew the straps to the bound-off edge of the back.

TO FINISH

Join side seams.

Straps. Using size US 3 (3¼ mm) needles and with RS facing, pick up and k 4 sts from first 4 bound-off sts of front top edge. Beg p row, st-st until strap measures 10[**10½**:11½:**12**] in. (25 [**27**:29:**30.5**] cm). Bind off. Picking up sts from last 4 bound-off sts of front top edge, work 2nd strap to match.

Using matching thread, sew on sequins by bringing needle up to RS through the center hole, threading on a small bead and taking needle back to WS. Tie the straps around back of your neck for a halter top or, if you prefer, sew the straps to the back of the top.

ABOUT THIS YARN

Lurex Shimmer is a fine, smooth chainette-construction yarn with a metallic look. It's a mix of 80% viscose and 20% polyester with approximately 104 yds. (95 m) to a 25 g (approx. 1 oz.) ball.

Sheepskin-look vest

A back, two fronts, no sleeves. This is a really simple garment, all in stockinette, with just a bit of shaping at the waist for a flattering fit. The tufted yarn used for the collar and edgings gives a natural effect like sheepskin when worked in reverse stockinette stitch. The front edgings and collar are picked up and worked in one piece for a neat finish.

ESTIMATED TIME TO COMPLETE
The 1st size vest took 12 hours to make.

ABOUT THESE YARNS
Rowan Big Wool is a soft, 2-ply 100% merino wool yarn with 87 yds. (80 m) to a 100 g (approx. 3½ oz.) ball. Big Wool Tuft is a highly textured mix of 97% merino wool and 3% nylon with 27 yds. (25 m) to a 50g (approx. 1¾ oz.) ball.

SIZES
To fit: bust 34 to 36[**38 to 40**:42 to 44] in. (86 to 91[**97 to 101.5**:107 to 112] cm)
Actual measurements: bust 37½[**41½**:45½] in. (95[**105.5**:116] cm); **length** 25[**26**:27½] in. (63.5[**66.5**:70]cm). Figures in square brackets refer to larger sizes; where there is only one figure, it refers to all sizes.

YOU WILL NEED
- 4(**5**:6) x 100 g balls (approx. 14[17½:21] oz.) of Rowan Big Wool in Latte, shade 018 (A)
- 2 x 50 g balls (approx. 3½ oz.) of Rowan Big Wool Tuft in Frosty, shade 055 (B)
- pair of size US 17 (12 mm) knitting needles
- 32-in. (81-cm)- long size US 17 (12 mm) circular needle
- one large button

GAUGE
8 sts and 12 rows to 4 in. (10 cm) over st-st, using Big Wool on size US 17 (12 mm) needles. Change needle size, if necessary, to obtain this gauge.

ABBREVIATIONS
beg = beginning; **cont** = continue; **dec** = decrease; **foll** = following; **inc** = increase; **kfb** = k into front and back of st; **k** = knit; **p** = purl; **RS** = right side; **skpo** = slip 1, k1, pass slipped st over; **sl** = slip 1 st purlwise; **st(s)** = stitch(es); **st-st** = stockinette st; **tog** = together; **WS** = wrong side.

NOTE
- The seam stitches have been deducted to give the actual bust measurement.

TIPS

- Before making the button loop and sewing on the button, try on the vest and mark the best place to fasten it.

- When picking up stitches, insert the needle through the knitting 1 stitch in from the edge.

- When picking up stitches for the armhole edgings, make sure you knit 19(**21**:23) sts evenly on each side of the shoulder seam.

Big needles and thick, soft yarn make this wonderful, long vest a short piece of work.

VEST
BACK

Using A, cast on 40(**44**:48) sts. Beg k row, st-st 10 rows.

Dec row (RS) K2, k2tog, k to last 4 sts, skpo, k2. 38(**42**:46) sts.
Cont in st-st, dec in this way at each end of 2 foll 4th rows. 34(**38**:42) sts.
St-st 7 rows.

Inc row (RS) K1, kfb, k to last 3 sts, kfb, k2. 36(**40**:44) sts.
Cont in st-st, inc in this way at each end of 2 foll 6th rows. 40(**44**:48) sts.
St-st 11 rows.

Shape armholes. Bind off 2 sts at beg of next 2 rows. 36(**40**:44) sts.
Dec in same way as before at each end of next 3(**4**:5) RS rows. 30(**32**:34) sts.
St-st 19(**21**:23) rows. Bind off.

LEFT FRONT

Using A, cast on 20(**22**:24) sts. Beg k row, st-st 10 rows.

Dec row (RS) K2, k2tog, k to end. 19(**21**:23) sts.
Cont in st-st, dec in this way at beg of 2 foll 4th rows. 17(**19**:21) sts.
St-st 7 rows.

Inc row (RS) K1, kfb, k to end. 18(**20**:22) sts.
Cont in st-st, inc in this way at beg

of 2 foll 6th rows. 20(**22**:24) sts.
St-st 11 rows.

Shape armhole and neck. Bind off 2 sts at beg of next row. 18(**20**:22) sts.
P 1 row.

Dec row 1 (RS) K2, k2tog, k to last 4 sts, skpo, k2. 16(**18**:20) sts.
Cont in st-st, dec in this way at each end of next 2(**3**:4) RS rows. 12 sts.
St-st 3 rows.

Dec row 2 (RS) K to last 4 sts, skpo, k2. 11 sts.
Cont in st-st, dec in this way at end of 3 foll 4th rows. 8 sts.
St-st 3(**5**:7) rows. Bind off.

RIGHT FRONT

Using A, cast on 20(**22**:24) sts. Beg k row, st-st 10 rows.

Dec row (RS) K to last 4 sts, skpo, k2. 19(**21**:23) sts.
Cont in st-st, dec in this way at end of 2 foll 4th rows. 17(**19**:21) sts.
St-st 7 rows.

Inc row (RS) K to last 3 sts, kfb, k2. 18(**20**:22) sts.
Cont in st-st, inc in this way at end of 2 foll 6th rows. 20(**22**:24) sts.
St-st 12 rows.

Shape armhole and neck. Bind off 2 sts at beg of next row. 18(**20**:22) sts.
Dec row 1 (RS) K2, k2tog, k to last 4 sts, skpo, k2. 16(**18**:20) sts.
Cont in st-st, dec in this way at each end of next 2(**3**:4) RS rows. 12 sts.
St-st 3 rows.

Dec row 2 (RS) K2, k2tog, k to end.
Cont in st-st, dec in this way at beg of 3 foll 4th rows. 8 sts.
St-st 3(**5**:7) rows. Bind off.

FRONT EDGINGS AND COLLAR

Matching sts, join shoulder seams.
Using circular needle B and with RS facing, pick up 36 sts up right front

to start of neck shaping, 17(**19**:21) sts up right front neck to shoulder, 14(**16**:18) sts across back neck, 17(**19**:21) sts down left front neck to end of shaping, and 36 sts down left front to lower edge. 120 (**126**:132) sts.
Leaving a 4-in. (10-cm) end, cut yarn.

Collar. Row 1 (WS) Using circular needle, slip 36 sts and leave these sts on needle for left front edging, p next 48(**54**:60) sts, turn and work collar on these sts, leaving 36 sts on needle or on a holder for right front edging.

Row 2 Sl 1, k45(**51**:57), turn and leave 2 more sts.

Row 3 Sl 1, p43(**49**:55), turn and leave 2 more sts.

Row 4 Sl 1, k41(**47**:53), turn and leave 2 more sts.

Row 5 Sl 1, p39(**45**:51), turn and leave 2 more sts.

Row 6 Sl 1, k37(**43**:49), turn and leave 2 more sts.

Row 7 Sl 1, p35(**41**:47), turn and leave 2 more sts.

Row 8 Sl 1, k33(**39**:45), turn and leave 2 more sts, leaving an end, cut yarn and slip 36 sts of left front edging onto needle.

Edging. Next row Bind off 36 sts of left front edging knitwise, 48(**54**:60) sts of collar purlwise and 36 sts of right front edging knitwise.

ARMHOLE EDGINGS

Using B and with RS facing, pick up 38(**42**:46) sts around each armhole edge. Bind off knitwise. Weave in yarn ends.

TO FINISH

Press according to yarn label. Join side seams. Using A, make button loop under right front edging just above waist level. Sew on button.

Dip-and-rip vest

First you dip-dye the fabric; then you rip it into strips, roll it into balls, and start knitting. The top is just stockinette stitch on supersize needles with the minimum of shaping, so it's really quick to do.

ESTIMATED TIME TO COMPLETE
Not counting dyeing and drying time, it took about an hour to rip the strips and 3 hours to knit the 1st size top: 4 hours total.

ABOUT THIS YARN
This is a "yarn" you make yourself, so you can vary the color and the thickness as you wish. Just make sure that you use 100% cotton fabric for your "yarn," as it will tear easily, creating lovely frayed edges, and will also wash and take dye well. The top in the photo at right was made from hand-dyed, loosely woven muslin.

SIZES
To fit: bust 34 to 36[**38 to 40**:42 to 44] in. (86 to 91[**97 to 101.5**:107 to 112] cm).
Actual measurements: bust 36½[**40½**:44½] in. (93[**103**:113] cm); **length** 19½[**21**:22] in. (49.5[**53.5**:56] cm). Figures in square brackets refer to larger sizes; where there is one figure, it refers to all sizes.

YOU WILL NEED
- 4½[**5⅛**:5⅞] yds. (4[**4.7**:5.4] m) of approximately 44-in.(112-cm)- wide soft unbleached muslin
- dye in color of your choice
- sharp scissors
- pair of size US 35 (20 mm) knitting needles

GAUGE
6 sts and 6 rows to 4 in. (10 cm) over st-st on size US 35 (20 mm) needles. Change needle size, if necessary, to obtain this gauge.

ABBREVIATIONS
beg = beginning; **cont** = continue; **dec** = decrease; **k** = knit; **p** = purl; **RS** = right side; **skpo** = slip 1, k1, pass slipped st over; **st(s)** = stitch(es); **st-st** = stockinette st; **tog** = together; **WS** = wrong side.

NOTES
- Fabric amounts needed may vary according to the weight and width of the fabric and the amount lost by fraying when ripping the strips.
- Dye the fabric before tearing it into strips.
- The stitches are so big that allowance has been made in the actual measurements for taking 1 stitch from each edge into the seams.

TIPS

- Choose a 100% cotton muslin fabric. It will rip more easily than a polyester mix (see About This Yarn, opposite).

- For a white top, simply buy bleached muslin.

- For a multi-colored top, buy several blending shades of dye. Start by dyeing with the lightest color first; then dry and retie the fabric between each different color.

Be truly creative and
make your own fabric
"yarn" to knit this
simple top.

PREPARING THE YARN

Wash the fabric to remove any sizing from it. To create a mottled effect, scrunch, fold, wrap, knot, or tie the fabric before dyeing it according to the instructions for the dye product you have chosen. Dry the fabric. Tear the fabric into lengthwise strips by snipping the cut or torn edge about ¾ in. (2 cm) in from the selvage, and ripping down the length until about 1 in. (3 cm) from the bottom. Now, starting from that edge, snip the fabric another ¾ in. (2 cm) along from the first tear, and rip again, stopping about 1 in. (2.5 cm) from the other end. Keep ripping strips in this way, turning the fabric upside down for each strip. Ripping along the length of the fabric gives you long strips; and because you do not rip right to the end, the strips are joined and can be wound into a ball. Although you're aiming for the strips to be about ¾ in. (2 cm) wide, it's not possible to snip and tear every strip exactly the same, and the fabric will fray at the edges, so your yarn may vary from ⅝ to 1 in. (1.5 to 2.5 cm). This won't matter, as long as you end up with around 130[**150**:175] yds. (120[**140**:160] m) of fabric "yarn."

VEST
BACK

Cast on 30(**33**:36) sts.
Beg k row, st-st 18 rows.
Shape armholes. Bind off 3 sts at beg of next 2 rows. 24(**27**:30) sts.
Dec row (RS) K2, k2tog, k to last 4 sts, skpo, k2. 22(**25**:28) sts.
Cont in st-st, dec in this way at each end of next 2 RS rows.
18(21:24) sts**.

St-st 5(**7**:9) rows. Leave sts on a stitch holder.

FRONT

Work as given for back to **.
St-st 0(**2**:4) rows.
Shape neck. Next row (WS) P5(**6**:7), turn and complete right side on these sts.
Dec row (RS) K1, k2tog, k to end. 4(**5**:6) sts.
Cont in st-st, dec in this way at beg of next RS row. 3(**4**:5) sts. P 1 row. Leave sts on a holder.
With WS facing, slip center 8(**9**:10) sts onto a holder, p to end. 5(**6**:7) sts.
Dec row (RS) K to last 3 sts, skpo, k1. 4(**5**:6) sts.
Cont in st-st, dec in this way at end of next RS row. 3(**4**:5) sts. P 1 row. Leave sts on a holder.

NECK EDGING

With RS of back and front together and back facing, taking 1 st from each side each time, bind off 3(**4**:5) sts of back tog with sts of left front shoulder. With RS facing and leaving 3(**4**:5) sts of back for right shoulder, slip center 12(**13**:14) sts of back onto right needle, pick up and k 5 sts down left front neck, k center 8(**9**:10) sts, pick up and k 5 sts up right front neck. 30(**32**:34) sts. Turn and bind off knitwise.

TO FINISH

Join right shoulder in the same way as left shoulder, then join ends of neck edging. Taking 1 stitch in from each edge, and using mattress stitch (see page 154), join side seams. Weave in yarn ends.

Shaded jacket

The bouclé yarn used for this jacket makes a dense, springy fabric with a fashionable felted look. What's more, it's easy to handle: The loops in the yarn are big enough to create a texture but small enough not to catch on the needles. The jacket is worked in stockinette stitch, so the cuffs and edging make a nice neat roll; and because of the all-in-one construction, there are only two seams to join.

ESTIMATED TIME TO COMPLETE
The 1st size jacket took 37 hours to make.

ABOUT THIS YARN
Yo-yo is an ultra-lightweight bouclé yarn that's a mix of 74% acrylic, 14% wool, and 12% polyester. The yarn is dyed to shade from dark to light to dark again within one extra-large, 400 g (approx. 14 oz.) ball. Each ball has approximately 960 yds. (880 m).

SIZES
To fit: bust 34 to 38[**40 to 44**] in. (86 to 97[**101.5 to 112**] cm).
Actual measurements: bust 47[**52½**] in (119[**133**] cm); **length** 23½[**24½**] in. (60[**62**] cm); **sleeve** 18 in. (46 cm). Figures in square brackets refer to larger size; where there is only one figure, it refers to both sizes.

YOU WILL NEED
• 1 x 400 g ball (approx. 14 oz) of Sirdar Yo-yo in Midnight Mood, shade 0016
• pair of size US 7 (4½ mm) knitting needles
• 32-in. (81-cm)- long size US 7 (4½ mm) circular needle

GAUGE
15 sts and 24 rows to 4 in. (10 cm) over st-st on size US 7 (4½ mm) needles. Change needle size, if necessary, to obtain this gauge.

ABBREVIATIONS
beg = beginning; **cont** = continue; **dec** = decrease; **foll** = following; **k** = knit; **kfb** = k into front and back of st; **p** = purl; **pfb** = purl into front and back of st; **RS** = right side; **skpo** = slip one, k1, pass slipped st over; **st(s)** = stitch(es); **st-st** = stockinette st; **tog** = together; **WS** = wrong side.

TIPS

● The jacket is knitted in one piece from cuff to cuff. Use the pair of needles for the sleeves, and change to the circular needle to accommodate the extra stitches for the back and front, working back and forth in the usual way.

● Take the yarn from the center of the ball. Although you need to fish to find the end, once you start knitting, it will unwind smoothly, instead of flopping around as it does when the yarn is pulled from the outside.

● Yo-yo makes such a textured fabric that it is hard to see the stitches. When working your gauge swatch, cast on 19 stitches and work in stockinette stitch for 28 rows. For the stitch gauge, place markers on the right side, 2 stitches in from each edge, and measure between markers. For the row gauge, place markers 2 rows in from each edge and measure between markers on the wrong side.

This relaxed-fit jacket is knitted in one piece from cuff to cuff. Depending on your style, you can wrap and pin the fronts, add a belt, or leave the jacket loose.

JACKET

Right sleeve. Cast on 40(**46**) sts.
Beg k row, st-st 14(**8**) rows.
Inc row (RS) K1, kfb, k to last 3 sts, kfb, k2. 42(**48**) sts.
Cont in st-st, inc in this way at each end of 15(**16**) foll 6th rows. 72(**80**) sts.
St-st 5 rows. Do not turn at end of last row.
Cast on 54 sts.
Back and front. Row 1 (RS) K 54 cast-on sts and 72(**80**) sts of sleeve, cast on 54 sts. 180(**188**) sts.
Beg p row, st-st 47(**53**) rows.
Right front. Row 1 (RS) K90(**94**), turn and complete right front on these sts.
Row 2 Bind off 2 sts, p to end. 88(**92**) sts.
Row 3 K to last 2 sts, skpo. 87(**91**) sts.
Work Rows 2 and 3 10(**11**) more times. 57(**58**) sts.
Bind off knitwise.
Back neck. With RS facing, join yarn at right shoulder and k to end. 90(**94**) sts.
Beg p row, st-st 47(**51**) rows, ending with a p row. Leave sts on a holder.
Left front. Cast on 57(**58**) sts.
Row 1 (RS) K.
Row 2 Pfb, p to end. 58(**59**) sts.
Row 3 K to end, cast on 2 sts. 60(**61**) sts.
Work Rows 2 and 3 10(**11**) more times. 90(**94**) sts.
P 1 row.
Joining row (RS) K90(**94**) sts of left front and 90(**94**) sts of back. 180(**188**) sts.
Beg p row, st-st 47(**53**) rows.
Left sleeve. Cont in st-st, bind off 54 sts at beg of next 2 rows. 72(**80**) sts.
St-st 4 rows.
Dec row (RS) K2, k2tog, k to last 4 sts, skpo, k2. 70(**78**) sts.

Cont in st-st, dec in this way at each end of 15(**16**) foll 6th rows. 40(**46**) sts.
St-st 13 (**7**) rows. Bind off.

TO FINISH

Edging. Using circular needle, pick up and k 57(**58**) sts up right front to start of neck shaping, 44(**48**) sts up right front neck, 36(**38**) sts across back neck, 44(**48**) sts down left front neck and 57(**58**) sts down left front to lower edge. 238(**250**) sts. Beg p row, st-st 5 rows. Bind off.
Join side and sleeve seams.
Weave in yarn ends.

TIPS

● Mark the sleeve increases and decreases with knotted loops of contrasting thread to help keep track of the rows between shaping.

● Leave the markers in place to help you match the sleeve edges when sewing them together.

● When counting rows, it's easier to count the ridges on the wrong side; if necessary, bump your thumbnail down them.

● The shading will take care of itself until you divide at the neck. When rejoining yarn at the back and for the left front, you can match the shading so there isn't a big jump in color by winding some yarn off. If necessary, use the spare yarn to complete the left sleeve and work the edging.

Circular sweater

The main reason why this sweater is so quick to knit is its ease of construction. When you work stockinette stitch in the round, all you do is knit; there are no purl rows to slow you down. If you're one of those people whose purl rows are noticeably deeper than her knit rows, you'll be pleasantly surprised at how even your work is. The other time-saver is the minimal finishing required: You have only two tiny underarm seams to sew up, and your sweater will be ready to wear!

ESTIMATED TIME TO COMPLETE
The 1st size sweater took 15 hours to knit.

ABOUT THIS YARN
Noro Kureyon is a hand-spun-look, pure wool roving yarn with 109 yds. (100 m) to a 50 g (approx. 1¾ oz.) ball. The colors are random dyed and shaded from bright to dark, which produces a splashy, striped effect when knitted.

SIZES
To fit: bust 34 to 36[**38 to 40**:42 to 44:**46 to 48**] in. (86 to 91[**97 to 101.5**:107 to 112:**117 to 122**] cm).
Actual measurements: bust 39½[**44** :48: **53**] in. (100[**112**:122:**134.5**] cm); **length** 22[**23½**:24:**25**] in. (56[**60**:61:**63.5**] cm); **sleeve** 19 in. (48 cm). Figures in square brackets refer to larger sizes; where there is only one figure, it refers to all sizes.

YOU WILL NEED
- 10(**12**:13:**15**) x 50 g balls (approx. 17½[**21**:22¾:**26¼**] oz.) of Noro Kureyon in shade 124
- 16-in. (40.5-cm) long size US 8 (5 mm) circular needle
- 24-in. (61-cm) long size US 8 (5 mm) circular needle
- set of double-pointed size US 8 (5 mm) needles

GAUGE
18 sts and 24 rows to 4 in. (10 cm) over st-st on size US 8 (5 mm) needles. Change needle size, if necessary, to obtain this gauge.

ABBREVIATIONS
cont = continue; **dec** = decrease; **foll** = following; **inc** = increase; **k** = knit; **kfb** = k into front and back of st; **p** = purl; **RS** = right side; **skpo** = slip 1, k1, pass slipped st over; **st(s)** = stitch(es); **st-st** = stockinette stitch; **tog** = together; **[ ]** = work instructions in square brackets as directed.

TIPS

- The sweater is worked in the round, from the neck downward, apart from a few rows worked back and forth when shaping armholes. This enables you to try on the sweater when it's partly finished and adjust the sleeve length, if necessary.

- Take care not to twist the stitches on the needle when joining the first round.

- Place a marker to show the beginning of the rounds.

- Use the circular needle to work back and forth in rows, leaving the other stitches unworked on the needle.

Once you learn to knit sweaters in the round, you may find it to be your favorite technique.

Vibrantly shaded yarn adds excitement to this incredibly simple sweater. Knitted almost entirely in the round, it's in stockinette stitch with little rolled edges and is gently shaped to skim the figure.

BODY

Collar. Using short circular needle, cast on 85(**85**:90:**90**) sts. K every round for st-st until collar measures 8 in. (20 cm).

Shape yoke. Change to longer circular needle when necessary.

Inc Round 1 [Kfb, k3, kfb] 17(**17**:18:**18**) times. 119(**119**:126:**126**) sts.
K 2 rounds.

Inc Round 2 [Kfb, k5, kfb] 17(**17**:18:**18**) times. 153(**153**:162:**162**) sts.
K 4 rounds.

Inc Round 3 [Kfb, k7, kfb] 17(**17**:18:**18**) times. 187(**187**:198:**198**) sts.
K 4 rounds.

Inc Round 4 [Kfb, k9, kfb] 17(**17**:18:**18**) times. 221(**221**:234:**234**) sts.
K 4 rounds.

Inc Round 5 [Kfb, k11, kfb] 17(**17**:18:**18**) times. 255(**255**:270:**270**) sts.
K 4 rounds.

Inc Round 6 [Kfb, k13, kfb] 17(**17**:18:**18**) times. 289(**289**:306:**306**) sts.

2nd size only K 4 rounds.
Inc Round 7 [Kfb, k15, kfb] 17 times.
3rd and 4th sizes only K 4 rounds.
Inc Round 7 [Kfb, k15, kfb] 18 times.
4th size only K 4 rounds.
Inc Round 8 [Kfb, k17, kfb] 18 times.
All sizes 289(**323**:342:**378**) sts.
K every round in st-st until yoke measures 8 [**9**:9½:**10¼**] in. (20[**23**:24:**26**] cm) from inc round 1.

Shape armholes. The yoke is divided, and the back and front are worked in rows while increasing to shape the armholes, then joined again to work the body in rounds. The stitches for the sleeves are left until later.

Row 1 of back (RS) Sl 1, k84(**94**:102:**113**), turn and leave 205(**229**:240:**265**) sts for sleeves and front. P 1 row.

Inc row (RS) Kfb, k to last 2 sts, kfb, k1. 86(**96**:104:**115**) sts.

Cont in st-st, inc in this way at each end of next 2(**2**:3:**3**) RS rows. 90(**100**:110:**121**) sts. Break yarn and leave sts on needle.

Slip next 60(**67**:69:**76**) sts onto a holder for left sleeve.

Row 1 of front (RS) K next 85(**95**:102:**113**) sts, turn and leave remaining 60(**67**:69:**76**) sts on a holder for right sleeve. P 1 row.

Inc in same way as back at each end of next row and on foll 2(**2**:3:**3**) RS rows. 91(**101**:110:**121**) sts.

Body. Joining round (RS) K 90(**100**:110:**121**) sts of back and 91(**101**:110:**121**) sts of front. 181(**201**:220:**242**) sts.

K 24 rounds.

Dec Round 1 K1, k2tog, k84(**94**:104:**115**), skpo, k2, k2tog, k85(**95**:104:**115**), skpo, k1. 177(**197**:216:**238**) sts.

K 7 rounds.

Dec Round 2 K1, k2tog, k82(**92**:102:**113**), skpo, k2, k2tog, k83(**93**:102:**113**), skpo, k1. 173(**193**:212:**234**) sts.

K 7 rounds.

Dec Round 3 K1, k2tog, k80(**90**:100:**111**), skpo, k2, k2tog, k81(**91**:100:**111**), skpo, k1. 169(**189**:208:**230**) sts.

K 7 rounds.

Dec Round 4 K1, k2tog, k78(**88**:98:**109**), skpo, k2, k2tog, k79(**89**:98:**109**), skpo, k1.

165(**185**:204:**226**) sts.

K every round until sweater measures 22[**23½** :24:**25**] in. (56[**60**:61:**63.5**] cm) from inc round 1 of yoke. Bind off.

SLEEVES

With RS facing, k 60(**67**:69:**76**) sts from left sleeve holder. P 1 row. Inc in same way as back at each end of next row and on foll 2(**2**:3:**3**) RS rows. 66(**73**:77:**84**) sts. Change to double-pointed needles.

Round 1 K22(**24**:25:**28**) sts on first needle, 22(**24**:26:**28**) sts on second needle, and 22(**25**:26:**28**) sts on 3rd needle. 66(**73**:77:**84**) sts.

K 6 rounds.

Dec round K1, k2tog, k to last 3 sts, skpo, k1. 64(**71**:75:**82**) sts.

Cont to k every round in st-st, dec in this way on 6(**9**:10:**12**) foll 8th rounds. 52(**53**:55:**58**) sts.

K every round until sleeve measures 19 in. (48 cm) from Round 1. Bind off.

Work right sleeve in the same way.

TO FINISH

Press according to yarn label. Join underarm seams. Weave in yarn ends.

TIPS

● If you prefer, you could use a very short circular needle to work the sleeves instead of double-pointed needles, or you could use long double-pointed needles throughout.

● Use the spare circular needle as a stitch holder.

● Placing a marker before each section on the first increase round of the yoke will cut down the counting time on the following increase rounds. Just slip the markers each time on the rounds in between.

● Use a different-colored marker for the beginning of the round so you don't accidentally take it out when moving markers.

● It's easy to keep track of the rounds between shaping if you mark each increase and decrease round as you work.

● Leave a marker on the first increase round of the yoke so you can immediately see where to start measuring when checking the length.

Blanket jacket

The patterning on this jacket looks complex, but actually it's just stockinette-stitch stripes with giant cross-stitches embroidered afterward. Knitting in the front bands and collar gives the jacket a neat finish, with the added bonus of avoiding a tiresome sewing job.

ESTIMATED TIME TO COMPLETE

The 1st size jacket took about 8 hours actual knitting time, plus 7 hours for the embroidery: 15 hours total.

ABOUT THIS YARN

Rowan Big Wool is an incredibly thick, soft, 2-ply, lightly twisted 100% merino wool yarn with 87 yds. (80 m) to a 100 g (approx. 3½ oz.) ball.

SIZES

To fit: bust 32 to 36[**38 to 42**:44 to 48] in. (81 to 91[**97 to 107**:112 to 122) cm
Actual measurements: bust 44[**48**:52½] in. (112[**122**:133] cm); **length** 26[**26¾**:27½] in. (66[**68**:70] cm); **sleeve** 16½ in. (42 cm). Figures in square brackets refer to larger sizes; where there is only one figure, it refers to all sizes.

YOU WILL NEED

- 4(**5**:5) x 100g balls (approx. 14[17½:17½] oz.) of Rowan Big Wool in Pip, shade 015 (A)
- 3(**4**:4) x 100g balls (approx. 10½ [**14**:14] oz.) same in Wild Berry, shade 025 (B)
- 2(**3**:3) x 100g balls (approx. 7[**10½**:10½] oz.) same in Cassis, shade 024 (C)
- pair each of size US 17 (12 mm) and size US 19 (15 mm) knitting needles
- 4 buttons
- 2 x 50g balls (approx. 3½ oz) of Rowan Kid Classic in shade 819 (D) (optional)
- large tapestry needle

GAUGE

7½ sts and 10 rows to 4 in. (10 cm) over st-st on size US 19 (15 mm) needles. Change needle size, if necessary, to obtain this gauge.

ABBREVIATIONS

beg = beginning; **cont** = continue; **dec** = decrease; **foll** = following; **inc** = increase; **k** = knit; **kfb** = k into front and back of st; **p** = purl; **RS** = right side; **skpo** = slip 1, k1, pass slipped st over; **st(s)** = stitch(es); **st-st** = stockinette st; **tog** = together; **WS** = wrong side; **yo** = yarn over needle to make a st.

NOTE

- Use a separate ball of B for the front edging and collar, and separate balls of A and B for the pocket patch, twisting yarns when changing colors to link areas.

TIPS

- When working with big needles, you can knit faster and take the weight off your wrists by working with the end of the right needle tucked under your arm.

- If you'd like to knit the jacket in just one color, follow the instructions, omitting the color changes. You'll need approximately 9(**10**:11) x 100 g balls (approx. 31½[**35**:38½] oz.) of Big Wool in your chosen color.

- If you don't want brightly contrasting embroidery, use Big Wool yarn colors leftover from knitting the jacket instead.

- When sewing together a garment with stitches as big as these, it really is important to join the seams with the right side facing, carefully using mattress stitch (see page 154) and taking 1 stitch in from each side.

This generously sized,
strikingly patterned
jacket is soft and cozy.

JACKET
BACK
Using size US 17 (12 mm) needles and B, cast on 44(**48**:52) sts.
K 4 rows.
Change to size US 19 (15 mm) needles. Beg k row, st-st stripes of 3 rows C, 11 rows A, 4 rows B, 8 rows A, 6 rows C, 4 rows B, 3 rows C, and 3 rows A. Cont in st-st and A.
Shape armholes. Bind off 3(**4**:5) sts at beg of next 2 rows. 38(**40**:42) sts.
Dec row (RS) K1, k2tog, k to last 3 sts, skpo, k1. 36(**38**:40) sts.
St-st 3 more rows in A. Cont in st-st stripes of 4 rows B, 3 rows C and 7(**9**:11) rows A. Cont in st-st and A.
Shape shoulders and back neck.
Bind off 3(**3**:4) sts at beg of next 2 rows.
Next row (RS) Bind off 4 sts, k until there are 7(**8**:8) sts on right needle, turn and complete right shoulder on these sts. Bind off 3 sts at beg of

next row. 4(**5**:5) sts. Bind off. With RS facing, bind off center 8 sts, k to end. 11(**12**:12) sts. Bind off 4 sts at beg of next row and 3 sts at beg of foll row. 4(**5**:5) sts. Bind off.

POCKET LININGS
(Make 2) Using US 19 (15mm) needles and C, cast on 10 sts. Beg k row, work 10 rows. Leave sts on a holder.

LEFT FRONT
Using size US 17 (12 mm) needles and B, cast on 24(**26**:28) sts.
K 4 rows.
Change to size US 19 (15 mm) needles.
Row 1 (RS) K 20(**22**:24) C, 4B.
Row 2 K4B, p20(**22**:24) C.
These 2 rows form st-st with k4B at front edge on every row.
Work 1 more row.
Row 4 (WS) K4B, p 5(**6**:7)A, 10C, 5(**6**:7)A.
Row 5 K 5(**6**:7)A, 10C, 5(**6**:7)A, 4B.
Work last 2 rows 4 more times, then work Row 4 again.
Change to B.
Pocket opening row (RS) K5(**6**:7), slip next 10 sts onto a holder and in their place k 10 sts of pocket lining, k to end.
Work 3 more rows B.
Cont in B for k4 front edging, work 8 rows A, 6 rows C, 4 rows B, 3 rows C, and 1 row A.
Shape collar and armhole.
Row 1 (RS) K19(**21**:23)A, using B, k3, kfb, k1. 25(**27**:29) sts.
Row 2 K6B, p19(**21**:23)A.
Row 3 Using A, bind off 3(**4**:5) sts, k until there are 16(**17**:18) sts in A on right needle, k6B. 22(**23**:24) sts.
Row 4 K6B, p16(**17**:18)A.
Row 5 Using A, K1, k2tog,

k12(**13**:14), using B, k5, kfb, k1.
Row 6 K8B, p14(**15**:16)A.
Row 7 K 14(**15**:16)A, 8B.
Row 8 K8B, p14 (**15**:16)A. Cont in B.
Row 9 K to last 2 sts, kfb, k1.
23(**24**:25) sts.
Row 10 K10, p to end.
K 1 row.
Row 12 K10, p to end.
Row 13 K12(**13**:14)C, using B, k9, kfb, k1. 24(**25**:26) sts.
Row 14 K12B, using C, p to end.
Row 15 K 12(**13**:14)C, 12B.
Row 16 K12B, using A, p to end.
Row 17 K11(**12**:13)A, using B, k11, kfb, k1. 25(**26**:27) sts.
Row 18 K14B, using A, p to end.
Cont in st-st and A with K14 in B for collar on every row, work 4(**6**:8) more rows.
Shape shoulder. Bind off 3(**3**:4) sts at beg of next row, 4 sts at beg of foll RS row and 4(**5**:5) sts at beg of next RS row. 14 sts.
Back collar. Cont in B on 14 sts, k every row until collar reaches center back neck. Bind off.

RIGHT FRONT
Using size US 17 (12 mm) needles and B, cast on 24(**26**:28) sts. K 4 rows.
Change to size US 19 (15 mm) needles.
Row 1 (RS) K4B, 20(**22**:24)C.
Row 2 P20(**22**:24)C, k4B.
These 2 rows form st-st with k4B at front edge on every row.
1st buttonhole row (RS) Using B, k1, k2tog, yo, k1, k20(**22**:24)C.
Row 4 P 5(**6**:7)A, 10C, 5(**6**:7)A, k4B.
Row 5 K4B, 5(**6**:7)A, 10C, 5(**6**:7)A.
Work last 2 rows 4 more times, then work Row 4 again. Change to B.
Pocket opening and 2nd buttonhole row (RS) K1, k2tog, yo,

k6(**7**:8), slip next 10 sts onto a holder and in their place k 10 sts of pocket lining, k to end.

Work 3 more rows B.

Cont in B for k4 front edging, work 8 rows A.

3rd buttonhole row (RS) Using B, k1, k2tog, yo, k1, using C, k to end. Cont in B for k4 front edging work 5 more rows C, 4 rows B, and 2 rows C.

4th buttonhole row (RS) As 3rd buttonhole row.

Next row K4B, using A, p to end.

Shape collar and armhole.

Row 1 (RS) Using B, kfb, k4, k19(**21**:23)A. 25(**27**:29) sts.

Row 2 P19(**21**:23)A, k6B.

Row 3 K 6B, 19(**21**:23)A.

Row 4 Using A, bind off 3(**4**:5) sts, p to last 6 sts, k6B. 22(**23**:24) sts.

Row 5 Using B, kfb, k6, using A, k to last 3 sts, skpo, k1.

Row 6 P14(**15**:16)A, k8B.

Row 7 K 8B, 14(**15**:16)A.

Row 8 P14(**15**:16)A, k8B. Cont in B.

Row 9 Kfb, k to end. 23(**24**:25) sts.

Row 10 P13(**14**:15), k10.

K 1 row.

Row 12 P13(**14**:15), k10.

Row 13 Using B, kfb, k10, k12(**13**:14)C. 24(**25**:26) sts.

Row 14 Using C, p to last 12 sts, k12B.

Row 15 K 12B, 12(**13**:14)C.

Row 16 Using A, p to last 12 sts, k12B.

Row 17 Using B, kfb, k12, k11(**12**:13)A. 25(**26**:27) sts.

Row 18 Using A, p to last 14 sts, k14B.

Cont in st-st and A with k14 in B for collar on every row, work 5(**7**:9) more rows.

Shape shoulder. Bind off 3(**3**:4) sts at beg of next row, 4 sts at beg of foll WS row, and 4(**5**:5) sts at beg of next WS row. 14 sts.

Back collar. Cont in B on 14 sts, k every row until collar reaches center back neck. Bind off.

SLEEVES

Using size US 17 (12 mm) needles and B, cast on 22(**24**:26) sts. K 4 rows. Change to size US 19 (15 mm) needles.

Beg k row, st-st 10 rows A.

Change to B. St-st 2 rows.

Inc row Kfb, k to last 2 sts, kfb, k1. 24(**26**:28) sts. P 1 row B.

Change to A. Cont in st-st, inc in same way as before at each end of Row 3 and foll Row 4. P 1 row. 28(**30**:32) sts.

Change to C. Inc as before at each end of Row 3. St-st 3 rows. 30(**32**:34) sts.

Change to B. Inc as before at each end of Row 3. 32(**34**:36) sts. P 1 row.

Change to C. St-st 3(**2**:2) rows.

2nd and 3rd sizes only Inc as before at each end of next row.

All sizes Cont in A. St-st 3(**3**:1) rows.

3rd size only Inc as before at each end of next row. P 1 row.

All sizes 32(**36**:40) sts.

Shape top. Bind off 3(**4**:5) sts at beg

of next 2 rows. 26(**28**:30) sts.

Next row (RS) Slipping first st, bind off 2 sts, k to last 2 sts, skpo.

Next row Slipping first st, bind off 2 sts, p to last 2 sts, p2tog. 20(**22**:24) sts. Bind off.

POCKET TOPS

Using size US 17 (12 mm) needles and B, k 10 sts from holder. K 4 more rows. Bind off.

TO FINISH

Press according to yarn label. Join shoulders. Join back collar seam, and sew row ends of collar to back neck. Set in sleeves. Join side and sleeve seams. Slip stitch pocket linings in place.Sew down ends of pocket tops. Sew on buttons. Weave in yarn ends Add embroidery. Using 4 strands of D and tapestry needle, work large cross-stitches over the stripes and overcasting stitches at each side of pockets and where A changes to C.

Bags

This collection of 12 designs includes little bags and big bags, boxy bags, and evening bags. Many of the designs are made from straight pieces of knitting. Pick a bag in ultra-thick yarn if you're looking for something speedy. For going shopping, choose the knit-in-the-round tote or string bag. If you're looking for a first-ever project, go for the mini-bag; it uses scrap yarn (get some from a knitter friend) and couldn't be simpler. There are bags with textured-stitch patterns and bags made from tweed, denim, and chenille. Finishing touches can make all the difference: Decorate your bags with vintage buttons or fringe, a pin or a clasp, a leather handle or a beaded handle. Improvise from the ideas shown here to personalize your bags.

- Denim bag
- Chunky-knit tote
- Weekend bag
- Gold sequin bag
- Moss-stitch bag
- String bag
- Knitting bag
- Woven-look bag
- Beaded cell-phone pouch
- Tweed handbag
- Black velvet bag
- Scrap mini-bag

Denim bag

The knitting is easy using made-to-fade indigo yarn. Structure the bag with iron-on stiffening and add a recycled jeans pocket for the perfect casual bag.

ESTIMATED TIME TO COMPLETE
The bag took 10 hours to make.

SIZE
Width: 11 in. (28 cm); **height:** 8 in. (20 cm).

YOU WILL NEED
- 2 x 50 g balls (approx. 3½ oz.) of Elle True Blue 100% Indigo Cotton DK in shade 112
- pair of size US 6 (4 mm) knitting needles
- a jeans pocket
- 10½ x 17¼ in. (27 x 44 cm) heavyweight iron-on lining
- one 11¾ x 18½ in. (30 x 47 cm) and two 4 x 9 in. (10 x 23 cm) pieces of matching sewing thread, sharp sewing needle, and tapestry needle
- 10½ x 17¼ in. (27 x 44 cm) and 36 in. (91 cm) of 1-in. (25-mm) wide iron-on adhesive
- 2 metal swivel trigger hooks and 2 metal D rings

GAUGE
22 sts and 30 rows to 4 in. (10 cm) over st-st on US 6 (4 mm) needles. Change needle size, if necessary, to obtain this gauge.

ABBREVIATIONS
beg = beginning; **k** = knit; **RS** = right side; **st (s)** = stitch (es) ; **st-st** = stockinette stitch; **WS** = wrong side.

NOTE
- Elle True Blue is a made-to-fade yarn that shrinks by approximately 5% when washed for the first time.

BAG
OUTER LAYER
Cast on 62 sts.
Beg k row, st-st until work measures 18 in. (46 cm), ending with a k row. Bind off knitwise.

SIDE PANELS
(Make 2) Cast on 15 sts. Beg k row, st-st until work measures 8¾ in. (22 cm), ending with a k row. Bind off knitwise.

HANDLE
Cast on 15 sts. Beg k row, st-st until work measures 15¾ in. (40 cm). Bind off.

TO FINISH
Wash and dry bag pieces. Placing pocket centrally, a few rows below one edge, sew pocket to RS of bag. Leaving 1 stitch at each side and cast-on and bind-off edges free, fuse the heavyweight iron-on lining to the WS of the outer layer of the bag. Using matching sewing thread and a sharp sewing needle taking in ½-in. (1.5-cm) seams, sew lining side panels to lining. Fold top hem down to WS, press in place, and using the iron-on adhesive, fuse WS of lining to WS of outer bag. With RS facing and using knitting yarn, a tapestry needle, and mattress stitch (see page 154), join knitted side panels to free stitch at each side of outer bag. Using matching sewing cotton and a sharp sewing needle, slip stitch top edge of lining to top edge of bag. Pin handle to ironing board, stretching it as much as possible, so the edges fold inward. Place doubled strip of iron-on adhesive inside curled handle and pin at each end to hold in place while fusing adhesive to flatten handle and secure folded-in edges. Sew D rings on each side of the top. Sew ends of handle to swivel trigger hooks. Fasten trigger hooks through D rings.

ABOUT THIS YARN
Elle True Blue is a double-knitting weight 100% cotton yarn dyed with environmentally safe indigo. It has 118 yds. (108 m) to a 50g (approx. 1¾ oz.) ball.

Casual and capacious, this bag is bound to become one of your all-time favorites.

TIPS

● Don't use fabric softener when washing the knitted pieces; some types of iron-on lining won't stick very well.

● Cut the fabric of the jeans close to the pocket to keep the stitching around the pocket intact. Trim off the fabric inside the pocket so only a tiny raw edge is left before sewing the pocket onto the outer bag.

● The sample bag was entirely hand-sewn. If you are confident with a machine, you could reduce the finishing time.

● Heavyweight fusible lining is usually sold to stiffen collars or curtain tiebacks. If you can get only lightweight fusible lining, use two pieces, one to stiffen the outer bag and the other to stiffen the lining fabric before making up the lining and fusing the lining to the outer bag.

● If you can't find trigger hooks in a department store, try a pet accessories shop; the hooks are often used on dog leads.

Flat knitting or round knitting—the choice is yours. Whichever you do, the bag won't take long; your balls of yarn will transform into this stylish carryall in just 4 hours.

Chunky-knit tote

You can knit this bag in the round or as two pieces. Knitting in the round feels like magic: Because you're always working on the right side, you can produce stockinette stitch without ever having to purl.

ESTIMATED TIME TO COMPLETE
The bag in the round took 4 hours to knit.

SIZE
Width: 17¼ in. (44 cm); **height:** 13 in. (33 cm).

YOU WILL NEED
- 5 x 100 g balls (approx. 17½ oz.) of Sirdar Bigga in Etna, shade 671
- If working in the round: 32-in. (81-cm) long size US 17 (12 mm) circular needle
- If working in 2 pieces: a pair of size US 17 (12 mm) needles
- large crochet hook

GAUGE
7½ sts and 10 rows to 4 in. (10 cm) over st-st on size US 17 (12 mm) needles. Change needle size, if necessary, to obtain this gauge.

ABBREVIATIONS
beg = beginning; **cont** = continue; **k** = knit; **p** = purl; **RS** = right side; **st(s)** = stitch(es); **st-st** = stockinette stitch; **[ ]** = work instructions in square brackets as directed.

TIPS

- If you are knitting the bag in the round, join in each new ball of yarn by knotting the ends. Use a square knot (that's right over left and under, left over right and under) to make a neat, flat knot. Pull hard to make sure the knot is tight; then, as you knit, make sure the ends are on the wrong side. Trim the ends.

- If you are knitting the bag in two pieces, join new balls of yarn at the sides.

BAG IN THE ROUND
Using circular needle, cast on 66 sts. Turn and k 1 row. Making sure that sts are not twisted on needle, join in a round and k every row in st-st until bag measures 13 in. (33 cm).
Shape base. Next round [Bind off 6 sts, k until there are 27 sts] twice. Cont on 27 sts for first side, turn and beg with a p row, st-st 4 rows. Leave sts on needle. Work 2nd side to match.

TO FINISH
With RS together, using a spare needle and taking 1 st from each side together each time, bind off.

Sew row ends to bound-off sts at each side of base. Weave in ends. Thread a length of yarn through cast-on edge, draw up slightly, and secure ends. This will strengthen the top edge and stop it from curling.
Handles. Mark a st each side of center 15 sts of one side of bag. Make a core for the handle: Thread yarn through top of bag at one marker, then thread through bag at other marker, leaving a 20-in. (51-cm.) loop. Repeat until core for handle has 6 strands. Overlapping ends at top of handle, cut yarn. Using a large crochet hook, work a row of single crochet over this core. Fasten off and

weave in yarn ends. Repeat for other handle.

BAG IN TWO PIECES
1st side Cast on 35 sts. Beg with a k row, st-st until side measures 13 in. (33 cm).
Shape base. Bind off 4 sts at beg of next 2 rows. 27 sts. St-st 4 rows. Leave sts on a holder.
2nd side Work as given for 1st side.

TO FINISH
Join base sts in same way as bag in the round. Join side seams and sew row ends to bound-off sts at each side of base. Make handles in same way as given for bag in the round.

ABOUT THIS YARN
Sirdar Bigga is a 50% wool, 50% acrylic, thick and soft, super-bulky yarn. There are about 44 yds.(40 m) per ball. The colorway shown here is dyed with short bursts of pink, brown, and natural, creating a speckled effect (see page 157 for resources).

Weekend bag

Knitting the outer layer of the bag is easy to do—it's all just simple shapes in stockinette stitch. Adding a fabric lining, zippers, click fasteners, and pocket detail takes a little more time but gives an authentic holdall style.

MAKING TIME
The bag took 13½ hours to make, including the lining and making up.

ABOUT THIS YARN
Sirdar Bigga is a super-chunky yarn that's a mix of 50% acrylic and 50% wool. It has 44 yds (40 m) to each 100 g (approx. 3½ oz.) ball.

SIZE
Width 19 in. (48 cm); **height** 13½ in. (34 cm); depth 9 in. (23 cm).

YOU WILL NEED
- 8 x 100 g balls (approx. 28 oz.) of Sirdar Bigga in Nocturne, shade 677
- pair of size US 19 (15 mm) knitting needles
- set of size US 10 (6 mm) double-pointed needles
- 1 x 12 in. (30.5 cm) and 1 x 26 in. (66 cm) heavyweight plastic zippers
- 59 in. (150 cm) of 1¼-in. (3-cm) wide strong cotton tape
- 2 plastic click fasteners
- 39½ in. (100.5 cm) x 61½ in. (156 cm) firm cotton lining fabric, such as light canvas or denim
- sewing thread to match lining, and long, sharp pins
- 19 in. (48 cm) x 10 in. (25 cm) piece of stiff cardboard or hardboard

GAUGE
6 sts and 9 rows to 4 in. (10 cm) over st-st on size US 19 (15 mm) needles. Change needle size, if necessary, to obtain this gauge.

ABBREVIATIONS
beg = beginning; **cont** = continue; **k** = knit; **p** = purl; **RS** = right side; **st(s)** = stitch(es); **st-st** = stockinette st; **tog** = together; **WS** = wrong side.

NOTES
- The measurements allow for 1 stitch to be taken into each seam.
- You will need only three of the double-pointed needles for the handles.
- If you set the pocket zipper in with a sewing machine, back the knitting with Stitch 'n' Tear or with tissue paper so that the knit fabric doesn't get caught in the feeder teeth.
- The handles are knitted in the round, enclosing the tape as you work. This makes them strong and seamless and saves threading the tape through a narrow tube of knitting.
- Check all lining measurements against the knitted pieces before cutting and adjust, if necessary, if your tension is not quite correct.

TIPS

- It's fine to use open-ended zippers. Although you don't need to undo the ends when using the bag, it's easier to set in the zippers if you can separate them for sewing after pinning them in place.

- Always set pins in at right angles to the zipper teeth, it holds the layers in place without slipping and makes it easy to remove the pins or even work right over them if you are machining the zipper in place.

- You can hand sew the whole bag but if you have a machine, then use it to sew the lining and set the longer zipper into the lining, and to set in the top edge of the pocket zipper.

- If you make the base board lining a really tight fit, the tucked-in end will be sure to stay in place without being stitched.

- There will be enough lining fabric left to line the pocket if you want. Just cut a piece of lining fabric 12 in. (30.5 cm) x 12 in. (30.5 cm), fold it in half, and sew each side seam. Insert lining into pocket, fold down top edges to fit, and slip-stitch to cover zipper fabric.

BAG

BACK

Using size US 19 (15 mm) needles, cast on 31 sts.
Beg k row, st-st 33 rows.
Bind off knitwise.

POCKET LINING

Using size US 19 (15 mm) needles, cast on 17 sts.
Beg k row, st-st 13 rows. Leave sts on a holder.

FRONT

Using size US 19 (15 mm) needles, cast on 31 sts.
Beg k row, st-st 12 rows.
Pocket opening row (RS) K7, bind off 16 sts purlwise, one st on right needle, return this st to left needle and k2tog, k6.
Pocket lining row P7, p17 sts of pocket lining, p7. 31 sts.
St-st 19 more rows.
Bind off knitwise.

SIDE PANELS

(Make 2) Using size US 19 (15 mm) needles, cast on 16 sts.
Beg k row, st-st 33 rows.
Bind off knitwise.

BASE

Using size US 19 (15 mm) needles, cast on 31 sts.
Beg k row, st-st 21 rows.
Bind off knitwise.

HANDLES

Cut tape in half to give 2 x 29½–in. (75-cm) lengths.
1st handle Using set of size US 10 (6 mm) needles, cast on 2 sts on first needle and 2 sts on 2nd needle, use 3rd needle to knit with and set 4th needle aside. Join the 2 needles to form a round and insert a length of tape in the center. As you knit, the tape will be covered. K every round for st-st until handle tube measures 21½ in. (55 cm). Bind off. Adjust tape so that approx. 4 in. (10 cm) shows at each end of the knitted tube.
2nd handle Work as given for 1st handle, checking that the length of the knitted tube is the same before binding off.

LINING

Cut 1 piece of lining fabric 39½ in. (100 cm) x 20 in. (51 cm) for the back, base and front lining, 1 piece 21 in. (53.5 cm) x 21 in. (53.5 cm) to cover the base board and 2 pieces 10½ in. (27 cm) x 14½ in (37 cm) for the side panels. If there is a RS to the lining fabric, make up the lining with the seams on the WS, taking ½ in. (1.5cm) into seams. Placing center of a shorter side of one side panel to center of one longer side of the back, base and front lining, set in first side panel. Set 2nd side panel into the other edge in the same way.

TO FINISH

Slip-stitch row-ends of pocket lining to WS of front. Set 12-in. (30.5-cm) zipper into pocket opening.With RS facing, using mattress stitch and taking 1 st from each edge into each seam, join front and back to side panels. Set in base of bag. Turn bag inside out and slip-stitch lower edge of pocket lining to base seam. Turn bag RS out. Placing WS of lining to WS of bag, starting at the corners and working up each seam, pin lining and bag together. Fold top edge of lining down to match height of bag and pin or tack in place. Remove pins holding lining in place and take out lining. With WS of lining facing, place front and back seams together and fold top edge in half. With zipper tag uppermost so zipper will be sandwiched between lining and bag, leaving a small space at each end, set in 26-in. (66-cm) zipper. Insert lining into bag and attach corners at lower edge of WS of lining to corners at base of WS of bag. Smooth knitted bag over lining, then insert handle ends through knitted fabric just above ends of pocket on front and in corresponding position on back, and pin tapes to lining. Check that the handles are level and that the tape ends don't show on the outside of the bag. Removing pins, sew tape at handle ends firmly to bag lining. Sew knitted handle ends to knitted bag.

With RS together, fold base board lining in half, check amount to take into seam to give a tight fit and sew seam. Refold lining so seam is in the center and sew along one short edge. Turn lining RS out and insert base board. Fold in excess and slip-stitch along edge to hold board in place. Open bag and fit base board into base of bag. Overlapping zipper fabric, pin, then sew cast-off edges of knitted bag in place to set in zipper. Fold ends of bag down to meet side panels and mark position for click fasteners just below the center of each panel. Sew one half of each click fastener to an end of top edge of bag and the other half on each side panel.

Chunky and capacious, this roomy bag will hold all you need for a weekend away.

Gold sequin bag

Sequin knitting is very effective and easier than it looks. You simply thread the sequins onto the yarn first, then just work in stockinette stitch, pushing a sequin through as needed—in this case, on every third stitch of alternate rows. It's not fast, because you have to slide the sequins up one at a time, but it's fascinating to do. If you knit with sequins over an entire garment, it does take a long time, but this little bag is really quick to make.

ESTIMATED TIME TO COMPLETE
The bag took 4 hours to knit, plus 1 hour for finishing: 5 hours total.

ABOUT THIS YARN
Coats Anchor Arista is a chain-construction metallic-look yarn that's a mix of 20% metal polyester and 80% viscose. It's lightweight but surprisingly strong and has 109 yds. (100 m) to a 25 g (approx. 1 oz.) ball.

SIZE
Width: 6 in. (15 cm); **length:** 4 in. (10 cm).

YOU WILL NEED
- 1 x 25 g ball (approx. 1 oz.) of Coats Anchor Arista in shade 300
- a strand of 1,000 ½-in. (12-mm) sequins or 361 loose ½-in. (12-mm) sequins
- pair of size US 2 (3 mm) knitting needles
- 6 x 8 in. (15 x 20 cm) heavyweight iron-on interlining
- 6¾ x 8¾ in. (17 x 22 cm) lining fabric
- matching sewing thread and sewing needle
- 6-in. (15-cm) lightweight "invisible" concealed zipper
- approximately 50 gold beads

GAUGE
26 sts and 39 rows to 4 in. (10 cm) over sequin patt on size US 2 (2¾ mm) needles. Change needle size, if necessary, to obtain this gauge.

ABBREVIATIONS
k = knit; **patt** = pattern; **p** = purl; **RS** = right side; **S1** = bring a sequin up close to back of work, then knit next stitch through back of loop, slipping sequin through stitch to lie on the front of the work; **[ ]** = work instructions in square brackets as directed.

NOTES
- Thread the sequins onto the yarn before starting to knit.
- Even though you don't need 1,000 sequins, it is worth buying a whole strand if you can, because they all face the same way on the strand, making it easier to thread them onto the yarn.
- The second side begins with the 3rd pattern row, so that the sequin pattern matches when you sew the side seams.

TIPS

- To thread sequins onto the yarn, thread a slim needle with a short length of sewing thread, knot the ends to form a loop, and slide the knot to one side. Pass the end of the yarn through the loop. Thread sequins, a few at a time, down the needle, over the loop, and onto the yarn.

- Sequins are very slightly cupped. They should be threaded onto the yarn with the convex side uppermost. If you thread them facing in different ways, they will reflect the light differently. If using a strand of sequins, simply check which way they face, carefully undo the knot in the strand, and slide a few at a time to the end of the strand and onto the needle. If working with loose sequins, check that they are facing the same way when you thread them.

- Do not press sequins, they will curl.

- If you can't find a 6-in. (15-cm) zipper, buy the nearest larger size and hide the end of the zipper between the bag and the lining.

- If you prefer, you could use a length of gold-colored chain instead of beads for the handle.

Just pop your evening essentials into this little bag, and you're ready to party.

BAG

1st side Cast on 39 sts. K 1 row. P 1 row. Work in sequin patt.

Row 1 (RS) K1, [S1, k3] to last 2 sts, S1, k1.

Row 2 P.

Row 3 K3, [S1, k3] to end.

Row 4 P.

These 4 rows form sequin patt. Patt 33 more rows, ending with Row 1. Bind off knitwise.

2nd side Work as given for first side, but begin and end with Row 3.

TO FINISH

Leaving ⅜ in. (1 cm) of lining free around each edge for seam allowances, fuse iron-on interlining to the wrong side of lining. With interlining facing, fold lining in half and join side seams. Join cast-on edges and side seams of bag. Set zipper into bound-off edges of bag, stitching as closely as possible to zipper teeth to hide zipper. Insert lining into bag, fold lining-fabric seam allowance down, and slip-stitch edges of lining close to zipper. For the handle, thread the beads onto a triple strand of yarn, knot ends, and sew on bag. Weave in yarn ends.

Moss-stitch bag

Thick yarn and big needles show up the stitches and make this a speedy project. The bag is knitted in three pieces: a front, a back that extends to make the flap, and a strap that also forms the gusset around the bag.

ESTIMATED TIME TO COMPLETE
The bag took about 3 hours to knit, including sewing it together.

ABOUT THIS YARN
Cargo is a 100% acrylic, thick chainette tube yarn with approximately 88 yds. (81 m) to a 100 g (approx. 3½ oz.) ball.

SIZE
Width: 10 in. (25 cm); **length:** 10 in. (25 cm); **depth:** 2¾ in. (7 cm).

YOU WILL NEED
- 3 x 100 g balls (approx. 10½ oz.) of Patons Cargo in Sassy, shade 10003
- pair of size US 15 (10 mm) knitting needles

GAUGE
10 sts and 12 rows to 4 in. (10 cm) over mst on size US 15 (10 mm) needles. Change needle size, if necessary, to obtain this gauge.

ABBREVIATIONS
cont = continue; **k** = knit; **mst** = moss stitch; **p** = purl; **RS** = right side; **st(s)** =stitch(es); **[ ]** = work instructions in square brackets as directed.

TIPS

- If you prefer, you could work to measurements. The front should measure 10½ in. (27cm) in length, the back and flap 16 in. (40.5 cm), and the strap 49 in. (124.5 cm).

- The strap stretches a little when worn.

- You could fasten the bag flap with a brooch or a decorative button and button loop.

FRONT
Cast on 27 sts.
Row 1 (RS) P1, [k1, p1] to end **.
This row forms moss st. Cont in mst for 32 more rows. Bind off knitwise.

BACK AND FLAP
As front to **. Cont in mst for 48 more rows. Bind off knitwise.

STRAP
Cast on 9 sts. Mst as given for front for 151 rows. Bind off.

TO FINISH
Join ends of strap. Placing this seam at the center of the cast-on edge and leaving approx. 17 in. (43 cm) for handle, join strap to lower edge and sides of front. Leaving approximately 5½ in. (14 cm) free at top edge for flap, join back to free edge of strap.

Moss stitch makes an interesting texture for this flap-over bag.

String bag

Transform ordinary parcel string into this tough bag. Working in the round makes the bag very strong, and the simple mesh stitch expands and stretches to hold masses of stuff.

ESTIMATED TIME TO COMPLETE
The bag took 2½ hours to make.

SIZE
Width: 15¾ in. (40 cm); **length:** 14 in. (35.5 cm).

YOU WILL NEED
- 2 x 128g spools (approx. 9 oz.) of medium-weight jute string
- 32-in. (81-cm)- long size US 19 (15 mm) circular needle
- size M/N or 13 (9 mm) crochet hook (optional)

GAUGE
6 sts and 5½ rounds to 4 in. (10 cm) over mesh patt, when stretched, using size US 19 (15 mm) circular needle. Change needle size, if necessary, to obtain this gauge.

ABBREVIATIONS
dec = decrease; **patt** = pattern; **p** = purl; **st(s)** = stitch(es); **tog** = together; **yo** = yarn over needle to make a stitch; **[ ]** = work instructions in square brackets as directed.

TIPS

- Take care not to miss out the first yarn-over at the beginning of rounds. You'll spot it quickly if you do, because the pattern will change.

- To join in more string, simply knot the ends. Use a square knot (that's right over left and under, left over right and under) so it will be flat. Pull the knot tight, and trim the ends short.

- Leave a long end when casting on, and use it as the base for the first handle.

This string shopping bag is ideal for fruit and vegetables.

BAG
Cast on 48 sts.
Round 1 [Yo, p2tog] to end.
This round forms mesh patt.
Work 16 more rounds.
Shape base. Dec round [P2tog] to end. 24 sts. P 1 round. Work dec round again. 12 sts.
Leaving a long end, cut the string. Thread end of string twice around through stitches; then knot the end of the string between each stitch, thread end under knots, and trim off.

TO FINISH
Handles. Thread string through cast-on edge of bag, then through again, about 5 in. (13 cm) farther along, to make a doubled loop 14 in. (35.5 cm) long as a base for first handle. Use crochet hook or your fingers to chain loops of string over base to make a firm handle. Leaving a short end, cut string and thread end under handle loops to secure it. Make second handle opposite first handle.

ABOUT THE YARN
The bag was made from medium-weight jute string with around 51 yds. (46 m) to a 128 g (approx. 4½ oz.) spool.

Knitting bag

You don't even need to know how to bind off to make this work bag. It's just two simple pieces of stockinette stitch sewn together and attached to handles. And it is strong, too, so you can use it for shopping and going out, as well as for your most important activity—knitting!

ESTIMATED TIME TO COMPLETE
The bag took 2½ hours to knit, including attaching the handles.

ABOUT THIS YARN
Sirdar Bigga is a 50% wool, 50% acrylic, thick and soft super-chunky yarn. It's really quick to knit and has 44 yds. (40 m) to a 100 g (approx. 1¾ oz.) ball.

SIZE
Width: 16½ in. (42 cm); **length:** 11¾ in. (30 cm) excluding handles

YOU WILL NEED
- 3 x 100 g balls (approx. 10½ oz.) Sirdar Bigga in Delta Blue, shade 688
- pair of size US 19 (15 mm) knitting needles
- tapestry needle
- pair of bamboo bag handles, approximately 12½ in. (32 cm) long

GAUGE
6 sts and 9 rows to 4 in. (10 cm) over st-st on size US 19 (15 mm) needles. Change needle size, if necessary, to obtain this gauge.

ABBREVIATIONS
beg = beginning; **k** = knit; **st(s)** = stitch(es); **st-st** = stockinette st.

TO FINISH
Join cast-on edges and side seams, leaving about 3¼ in. (8 cm) open at the top.

TIPS

● If you can't find ready-made handles, use 2 wooden dowels, cut to 12½ in. (32 cm) long, that have been sanded and varnished.

● If you're going to carry the bag around, make a lining from 2 pieces of cotton fabric, 17¾ x 12½ in. (45 x 32 cm). Join the pieces on one long and two short sides, leaving an opening at the top. Insert lining in bag, Turn in a ½-in. (1.5-cm) hem at the top edge of lining and slip stitch to the row below the gathered stitches.

BAG

1st side Cast on 27 sts. Beg k row, st-st 28 rows. Leaving an end about 3 yds. (2.5 m) long, cut yarn.
Attach handle. Knot yarn around the last stitch, thread a tapestry needle with the yarn end and slip the stitches, one at a time, off the needle and onto the yarn. Gather stitches slightly, and knot yarn around last stitch. Leaving about 2 in. (5 cm) of yarn between knitting and handle, wrap yarn tightly around handle; take it back through last stitch, then around the handle again. Work buttonhole stitches over yarn between handle and bag. Take end of yarn back through the knitted stitches again and fasten it to the first stitch. Attach the other end of the handle in the same way. Weave in yarn end and trim.
2nd side Work as given for first side.

Store your knitting projects in this easy-to-make bag.

Woven-look bag

The knitting is basically stockinette stitch; the woven effect is produced by picking up stitches and working in little blocks of 5 stitches and 8 rows. Once you've got the hang of picking up 1 whole stitch in from the edge, you'll find this a fascinating way of working. The blocks are tiny, so you can finish one in just a few minutes.

ESTIMATED TIME TO COMPLETE
The bag took 12 hours to make, including making the cord for the handle. Note: Beginners new to the technique may take longer to complete this project.

ABOUT THIS YARN
Noro Kureyon is a multicolored 100% wool single-twisted yarn with a hand-spun feel, with approximately 109 yds. (100 m) to a 50 g (approx. 1¾ oz.) ball.

SIZE
Width: 11¾ in. (30 cm); **length:** 13¾ in. (35 cm).

YOU WILL NEED
- 4 x 50 g balls (approx. 7 oz.) of Noro Kureyon in shade 40
- pair each of size US 7 (4½ mm) and size US 8 (5 mm) knitting needles

GAUGE
3 blocks measure 4 in. (10 cm) across; 5 lines of blocks measure 3½ in. (9 cm) when pressed, over entrelac patt on size US 8 (5 mm) needles. Change needle size, if necessary, to obtain this gauge.

ABBREVIATIONS
beg = beginning; **cont** = continue; **k** = knit; **kfb** = k into front and back of st; **p** = purl; **patt** = pattern; **RS** = right side; **skpo** = slip 1, k1, pass slipped st over; **st(s)** = stitch(es); **st-st** = stockinette stitch; **tog** = together; **WS** = wrong side.

NOTE
- Pick up stitches 1 whole stitch in from edge, spacing them on alternate row ends, so there are no gaps.

FIRST SIDE

Top edge. Using size US 7 (4½ mm) needles, cast on 36 sts. Beg p row st-st 9 rows.

Change to size US 8 (5 mm) needles. Work in entrelacs patt.

Base triangles. Row 1 (RS) K1, turn.

Row 2 P1.

Row 3 K2, turn.

Row 4 P2.

Row 5 K3, turn.

Row 6 P3.

Row 7 K4, turn.

Row 8 P4.

Row 9 K5, turn.

These 9 rows form the first base triangle and 1 st of 2nd base triangle. Work 2nd to 9th rows until 9 base triangles have been completed, ending last triangle k4.

1st line of blocks. The first side triangle is worked using 4 sts of the last base triangle.

1st side triangle. Row 1 (WS) P1, turn.

Row 2 Kfb. 2 sts.

Row 3 P1, p2tog, turn.

Row 4 K1, kfb. 3 sts.

The patchwork effect of this simple shoulder bag is achieved with a clever technique called "entrelac"—a French word meaning interlaced design.

Row 5 P2, p2tog, turn.

Row 6 K2, kfb. 4 sts.

Row 7 P3, p2tog, do not turn. First side triangle has been completed. Leave these 4 sts on needle.

1st block. Worked into 4 sts of next base triangle.

Purl 4 sts from row ends of previous base triangle, turn.

Row 1 (RS) K4.

Row 2 P3, p2tog, turn. Work Rows 1 and 2 3 more times, using all sts of base triangle.

Cont in this way, purling sts from row ends and working into next base triangle until 8 blocks have been completed.

2nd side triangle. Pearl 4 sts from row ends of last base triangle.

Row 1 (RS) K4.

Row 2 P2, p2tog. 3 sts.

Row 3 K3.

Row 4 P1, p2tog. 2 sts.

Row 5 K2.

Row 6 P2tog.

Row 7 K1 and leave this st on needle. 1st line of blocks has been completed.

2nd line of blocks. Worked into 1st line of blocks.

1st block With 1 st on right needle, pick up 3 sts from row ends of 2nd side triangle, turn. 4 sts.

Row 1 (WS) P4.

Row 2 K3, skpo, turn.

Work Rows 1 and 2 3 more times, using all sts of last block of 1st line of blocks.

Cont in this way, picking up 4 sts from row ends and working into next block each time until 9 blocks have been completed. Work next line of blocks as given for 1st line of blocks but using sts of 2nd line of blocks. Cont working lines of blocks into sts of previous line of blocks until 19 lines of blocks have been completed.

Closing triangles. Pick up 3 sts from row ends of last side triangle, turn. 4 sts.

Row 1 (WS) P4.

Row 2 K3, skpo, turn.

Row 3 P2, p2tog.

Row 4 K2, skpo, turn.

Row 5 P1, p2tog.

Row 6 K1, skpo, turn.

Row 7 P2tog.

Row 8 Skpo, do not turn.

With 1 st on right needle, pick up 3 sts from row ends of next block, turn. 4 sts.

Cont in this way working Rows 1 to 8 for each closing triangle.

Ending the last triangle at Row 7, fasten off.

SECOND SIDE

Work as given for first side.

TO FINISH

Join side and lower-edge seams. Using 10 lengths of yarn, each 3¾ yds. (3.5 m) long, make a twisted cord for handle—finished length approx. 40 in. (101.5 cm). Sew the cord to the bag.

Making a twisted cord. Tie the strands together at each end with an overhand knot. Dividing the strands into 2 groups of 5 each, slip one end over a door handle or a firmly fixed hook. Step back until the yarn is slightly stretched. Insert a pencil or small rod into the loop of yarn, and twist until the yarn starts to curl back on itself. With one hand, grasp the yarn at the center (a helper is useful for this) and take the rod end of the yarn to the fixed end. Holding these ends together, let go of the center. The yarn will twist around itself to make a cord. Still holding the ends firmly, smooth out any kinks, then tie an overhand knot to secure the ends; trim them to make a tassel about 3 in. (8 cm) long. Knot and trim the other end of the cord to match. See also page 155 for further instructions with diagrams.

See also page 155 for further instructions with diagrams.

TIPS

● You need to work quite a large sample in entrelac before you can measure it, so you may find it easier to check your stockinette stitch gauge, which should be 18 sts and 24 rows to 4 in. (10cm) on size US 8 (5 mm) needles.

● For a really hard-wearing bag, make a lining. Cut 2 pieces of cotton fabric, each 12½ x 15 in. (32 x 38 cm). Placing right sides together and taking ⅜-in. (1-cm) seam allowances, join both long sides and one short side. Insert lining into bag. Fold ½ in. (1.5 cm) of top edge of lining to wrong side, so that it is level with top of closing triangles, and slip stitch in place.

● If you want a twisted cord with 2 distinct strands of color, cut 5 lengths in one shade of the yarn and 5 in another. Knot the lengths together as usual, then keep the colors separate as you slip the yarn onto the hook. Arrange the loop of yarn so that the knots are level in the center and one color is at each end of the loop of yarn before you start to twist the strands together.

Beaded cell-phone pouch

Beaded knitting creates such a stunning effect that it really is worth the extra time spent threading the beads onto the yarn. For this bag, all you do is work in reverse stockinette stitch, sliding a bead up to hang between each stitch on the purl rows, where they will show up more than they would on knit rows. Instead of dealing with each bead separately, get into the habit of bringing several beads up on the yarn tensioned over the fingers, so you can flick one up close to the work when needed.

ESTIMATED TIME TO COMPLETE
The pouch took about 3 hours to knit, plus 1 hour to thread the beads: 4 hours total.

ABOUT THIS YARN
Rowan Lurex Shimmer is an 80% viscose, 20% polyester yarn with approximately 104 yds. (95 m) to a 25 g (approx. 1 oz.) ball. It's a fine yarn, so 1 ball goes a long way.

SIZE
Width: 2½ in. (6.5 cm); **length:** 4¾ in. (12 cm).

YOU WILL NEED
- 1 x 25 g ball (approx. 1 oz.) of Rowan Lurex Shimmer in Pewter, shade 333
- 725 small glass beads with diameter large enough to thread yarn
- pair of size US 2 (3 mm) knitting needles
- 2 larger glass beads, tapestry needle, and sharp sewing needle

GAUGE
21 sts and 40 rows to 4 in. (10 cm) over beaded rev st-st. Change needle size, if necessary, to obtain this gauge.

ABBREVIATIONS
B1 = bring 1 bead up close to work; **cont** = continue; **k** = knit; **p** = purl; **rev st-st** = reverse stockinette st; **RS** = right side; **st(s)** = stitch(es); **tog** = together; **WS** = wrong side; **[ ]** = work instructions in square brackets as directed.

NOTE
- Thread all beads onto yarn before starting to knit.

POUCH
Cast on 31 sts.
Row 1 (RS) [P1, B1] to last 2 sts, p2.
Row 2 K.
These 2 rows form beaded rev st-st. Work 47 more rows, so ending with a beaded row.
Drawstring channel. Cont in yarn without beads.
Next row (WS) P.
K 1 row. P 3 rows. K 1 row.
Next row (WS) P each st tog with corresponding st 6 rows down, at the same time, binding off each time there are 2 sts on right needle. Fasten off last st.

TO FINISH
Join side seam and cast-on edge. Use 4 x 48-in. (122-cm) lengths of yarn folded in half and twisted to make a cord (see page 155). Knot free ends and trim to make a small tassel, then thread on a large bead. Thread cord through drawstring channel. Thread other large bead, knot and trim to match first end.

Keep your cell phone in this pretty
drawstring pouch and you'll always
know where it is.

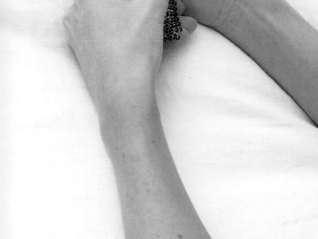

TIPS

● You can use any small glass beads
for the pouch; just make sure that the
hole in the beads is big enough so
you can thread them onto the yarn.

● Here's the easiest way to thread
the beads onto the yarn. First tip the
beads into a shallow dish, so they
don't spill all over the place. Thread a
slim, sharp needle with a short length
of sewing thread, knot the ends to
make a loop, and slide the knot up to
one side. Pass the end of the yarn
through the loop, pick up the beads
with the tip of the needle, and slide
them down over the loop and onto
the yarn.

● Tie the cord of the pouch to your
bag handle or your belt to keep your
cell phone handy.

● If you want to keep your cell phone
extra safe, you could line the pouch
with soft material.

● Phones are getting smaller all the
time. If you want to reduce the size of
the pouch, measure around your
phone, allowing for a little bit extra so
the pouch is not too tight, and cast on
4 sts fewer for each ¾ in. (2 cm)
smaller. For a shorter pouch, simply
work fewer rows. Don't forget that
you'll need fewer beads, too.

● You can also use the pouch to
store jewelry or your watch.

Tweed handbag

The outer layer of this bag couldn't be simpler; it's just three straight pieces of stockinette stitch. The trick is to use a really heavyweight iron-on interfacing to create a boxy shape that looks very professional. Adding a leather strap also helps turn "homemade" into "handmade."

ESTIMATED TIME TO COMPLETE
The bag took 5 hours to knit the pieces and 2½ hours to finish: 7½ hours total.

ABOUT THIS YARN
Debbie Bliss Aran Tweed is a flecked yarn with a hand-spun look. It's 100% wool and has approximately 109 yds. (100 m) to a 50 g (approx. 1¾ oz.) ball.

SIZE
Width: 11 in. (28 cm); **length:** 7 in. (18 cm); **depth:** 3 in. (7.5 cm)

YOU WILL NEED
- 3 x 50 g balls (approx. 5¼ oz.) of Debbie Bliss Aran Tweed in shade 07
- pair of size US 8 (5 mm) knitting needles
- 11 x 22 in. (28 x 56 cm) heavyweight iron-on interlining
- 11 x 22 in. (28 x 56 cm) and two pieces 3 x 7 in. (7.5 x 18 cm) iron-on bonding adhesive
- 11¾ x 23 in. (30 x 58.5 cm) lining fabric and 2 pieces 4 x 8 in. (10 x 20 cm)
- matching sewing thread and sewing needle
- leather belt to use as strap
- 2 small D rings
- 2 small single cap rivets
- Brooch or decorative button (optional)
- small amount of Debbie Bliss Cotton Cashmere in shade 18 and pair of size US 2 (2¾ mm) knitting needles for flower trim (optional)
- tapestry needle

GAUGE
18 sts and 24 rows to 4 in. (10 cm) over st-st on size US 8 (5 mm) needles. Change needle size, if necessary, to obtain this gauge.

ABBREVIATIONS
beg = beginning; **k** = knit; **RS** = right side; **st(s)** = stitch(es); **st-st** = stockinette stitch; **WS** = wrong side.

NOTE
- The instructions give both the number of rows and the length to knit. If you knit to the stated length, make sure you have the correct gauge, or you could need a different amount of yarn.

TIPS

- Instead of knitting a gauge swatch, cast on and knit one of the side pieces, counting the rows carefully. If it measures 3 in. (7.5 cm) wide by 7 in. (18 cm) long, you're doing well, and you'll be that much nearer to finishing.

- Steam-iron the knitted pieces for a slightly felted look.

- If you can't find a matching belt, use a short dog leash, recycle a handle from another bag, or knit a strap.

- For a really heavyweight iron-on interlining, look for the kind that's made to stiffen collars or furnishings.

Tweedy yarn gives a smart
look to this boxy bag.

the lining fabric of the bag. With RS
of bag facing, using a tapestry
needle, yarn, and mattress stitch
(see page 154), join the side bag
pieces to the main bag piece. Using
a sharp needle and matching sewing
thread, fold in edges of lining ½ in.
(1.5 cm) and slip stitch in place
around flap and top edge of bag.
Fasten belt and cut it in half. Cut a
small amount from each end, and
use to attach D rings. Slip ends of
belt through D rings and secure
them with the rivets. Pleat bag
sides, so the handle protrudes, and
sew pleats in place with a few hand
stitches. Fold down flap and
decorate with knitted flower or pin
to close.

BAG

Main piece. Using Aran Tweed and
size US 8 (5 mm) needles, cast on
52 sts.
Beg k row, st-st 133 rows, or until
work measures 22 in. (56 cm),
ending with a k row. Bind off
knitwise.

Side pieces. (Make 2) Cast on 16
sts. Beg k row, st-st 43 rows, or until
work measures 7 in. (18 cm), ending
with a k row. Bind off knitwise.

KNITTED FLOWER TRIM

Using cotton cashmere and size US
2 (2¾ mm) needles, work as given

for the flower trim on the floppy
brim hat (see page 35).

TO FINISH

Press according to yarn label.
Stretching knitting slightly, so that 1
stitch at each side and cast-on and
bound-off edges are free, fuse
heavyweight interfacing to WS of bag.
Leaving ½ in. (1.5 cm) free around all
edges, use iron-on bonding adhesive
to join lining to bag and to side
pieces. With RS of bag facing, and
leaving 4¾ in. (12 cm) at bound-off
edge of bag for flap, use a sharp
needle and matching thread to join
the lining fabric of the side pieces to

Black velvet bag

This bag is just one long strip of stockinette stitch, folded and seamed. The yarn is so thick and furry that when knitted at this gauge, it doesn't need a lining. Just add a cord for the handle, decorate it, and off you go!

ESTIMATED TIME TO COMPLETE
It took 7 hours to knit the bag, plus 1 hour to sew and decorate it: 8 hours total.

ABOUT THIS YARN
Sirdar Wow! is a super-thick 100% polyester chenille yarn with 64 yds. (58 m) to a 100 g (approx. 3½ oz.) ball.

SIZE
Width: 10½ in. (27 cm); **length:** 12 in. (30.5 cm) excluding fringe

YOU WILL NEED
- 3 x 100 g balls (approx. 10½ oz.) of Sirdar Wow! in Jet Black, shade 753 (A)
- pair of size US 10 (6 mm) knitting needles
- 1 x 100 g ball (approx. 3½ oz.) of Sirdar Pure Cotton 4-ply in Black, shade 41(B)
- assorted ½–2 in. (1.5–5 cm)-wide mother-of-pearl buttons
- 21-in. (54-cm) length of purchased fringe
- black sewing thread and sewing needle
- tapestry needle

GAUGE
11 sts and 14 rows to 4 in. (10 cm) over st-st on size US 10 (6 mm) needles. Change needle size, if necessary, to obtain this gauge.

ABBREVIATIONS
beg = beginning; **k** = knit; **st(s)** = stitch(es); **st-st** = stockinette st.

NOTE
- The gauge given here is tighter and the needle size is smaller than usual for Wow! to make a firm fabric for the bag.

TIPS

- Knot the end of the yarn before you start to knit to keep it from shedding.

- Always join in new yarn at the start of a row, never in the middle.

- To weave in yarn ends neatly, ease out the chenille fibers to leave a thin strand of thread, which will be easy to hide in the seam.

- Instead of using the chenille yarn, you may find it easier to sew the seams with sewing thread and a tapestry needle. Take 1 stitch in from each side to make a strong seam.

- If you don't want to make a cord, you can buy one instead. In this case, you won't need the 4-ply 100% cotton yarn.

- Instead of using mother-of-pearl buttons, you could decorate your bag with colored buttons, beads, or sequins.

BAG
Using A, cast on 30 sts.
Beg k row, st-st until bag measures 32½ in. (82 cm), ending with a k row. Bind off knitwise.

TO FINISH
Leaving 8½ in. (22 cm) free for flap, fold up lower 12 in. (30.5 cm) of bag and join side seams. Weave in the yarn ends.

Fold fringe in half, join ends, and sew along fold at lower edge of bag. Using 6 x 10-yds. (9-m) lengths of B doubled, make a twisted cord (see page 155) approximately 50 in. (127 cm) long with 5-in (13-cm) tassels of yarn after the knots at each end. Sew cord on bag for handle. Sew on buttons to decorate the bag flap, as shown at right.

Get that vintage look with this velvety bag decorated with mother-of-pearl buttons.

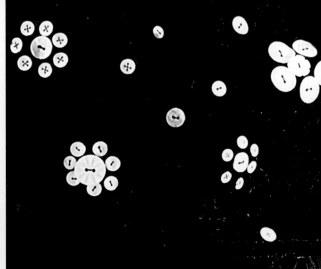

Scrap mini-bag

This sweet little bag is ideal for using up scraps, or an ideal learn-to-knit project for the young beginner. Using the DK yarn double with this size needles makes for a very firm surface. There are just 23 rows to knit, then you just finish it off with a twisted cord and it's ready to use.

ESTIMATED TIME TO COMPLETE
The bag took 1 hour to make.

ABOUT THIS YARN
Any pure wool or wool-mix DK yarn will do for the bag; the stripes use up even the smallest scraps.

SIZE
Width: 2¾ in. (7 cm); **length:** 2¾ in. (7 cm).

YOU WILL NEED
- approximately ½ oz. (15 g) of wool or wool-mix DK in black (A) and ⅓ oz. (10 g) in assorted colors (B)
- pair of size US 7 (4½ mm) knitting needles

GAUGE
16 sts and 32 rows to 4 in. (10 cm) using DK yarn double on size US 7 (4½ mm) needles. Change needle size, if necessary, to obtain this gauge.

ABBREVIATIONS
gst = garter st; **k** = knit; **patt** = pattern; **RS** = right side; **st(s)** = stitch(es).

NOTE
- Use yarn doubled throughout.

TIPS

- The easiest way to double the yarn is to use the end from the inside of the ball, along with the end from the outside of the ball together. Take care to include both strands as you form the stitches.

- The stripes make it easy to count the rows, as each ridge of color takes 2 rows.

- For a neat finish, simply weave the yarn ends in as you knit.

- You could make the bag in just two colors or even in one color.

BAG
Using A, cast on 24 sts.
Change to B. K 2 rows.
Change to A. K 2 rows.
These 4 rows form the gst stripe patt. Using a different color each time for B, work 19 more rows, ending with 1 row in A. Using A, bind off knitwise.

TO FINISH
Fold bag in half, and join cast-on edge for base and row ends for side seam. Cut 4 x 2¼-yds. (2-m) lengths in B, and knot ends together. Twist and double the yarn to make a cord handle. Knot the ends and trim to make tassels at each end of the cord. Sew the ends of cord to the sides of bag.

You'll find this little bag really useful for holding tickets and coins.

Knitting techniques

With just some yarn and two needles, you can create a wonderful, flexible fabric. All you need to know is how to cast on, make stitches, and bind off.

Once you've grasped the basics, you'll find projects in this book that you can get started on right away. Gain confidence from successful, simple knits, get comfortable with increasing and decreasing, then pick up a few finishing techniques and you can make anything you want.

THE BASICS

Casting on, knitting, purling, and binding off—these are the building blocks of the craft.

HOLDING THE YARN AND NEEDLES

Knitting is a two-handed craft. A needle is held in each hand, and the yarn is tensioned and manipulated with either the right or the left hand. The usual method of knitting is to work the stitches off the left needle onto the right needle. Some left-handers may prefer to reverse the direction of knitting; if you're left-handed, you could try using a mirror to reverse the diagrams. But most lefties find that holding the yarn in their left hand, so that it does more of the work, will solve the problem. Here's how most knitters hold the yarn and needles. However, there is no one correct method, so experiment until you find the way that's comfortable for you.

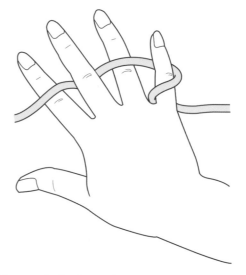

Yarn: right hand
The yarn leading to the work is on the left in this diagram, the yarn to the ball on the right. Catch the yarn around the little finger, then lace it over the third, under the middle, and over the first finger of the right hand.

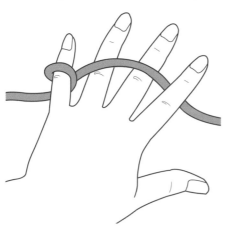

Yarn: left hand
The yarn leading to the work is on the right, the yarn to the ball on the left. Catch the yarn around the little finger, then take it over the third and middle fingers.

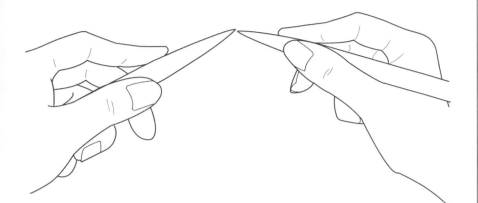

Right needle: like a pen

Pick up a needle with your left hand, holding it lightly over the top. Take the other needle in your right hand, holding it like a pen, with thumb and first finger lightly gripping it close to the tip and the shaft of the needle resting in the crook of your thumb. When you knit, slide the right hand forward, still supporting the needle.

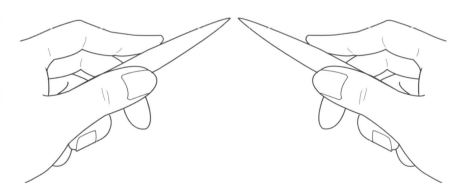

Right needle: like a knife

Pick up a needle in each hand, holding both needles lightly over the top. Tuck the end of the right needle under your arm. When you knit, let go of the needle and bring the right hand forward to manipulate the yarn, then return the fingers to the needle tip to move the stitches along.

MAKING A SLIP KNOT

Making a slip knot on the needle is the first step in knitting.

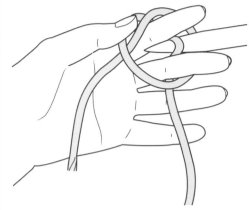

1. Wrap and pull through

Leaving the yarn end to the left and with the yarn to the ball on the right, wrap yarn loosely around the first two fingers of left hand, crossing over once. Insert the needle under the back strand, as shown, and pull through to make a loop.

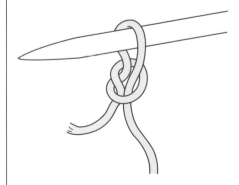

2. Tighten on needle

Slip fingers out and gently pull the end on the left to tighten the knot and the end on the right to close the loop on the needle.

CASTING ON

KNITTING OFF THE THUMB

I always recommend this as the easiest and most versatile method of casting on. It involves knitting into a loop around the thumb to make a stitch on the needle. The action is the same as making a knit stitch.

Start by leaving a long end, about three times the finished width of the knitting, and making a slip knot on the needle. The slip knot counts as the first stitch. Repeat steps 1 to 3 to cast on more stitches.

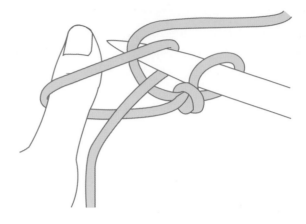

2. Yarn around needle

Bring the ball yarn up between thumb and needle, and take it around the needle, as shown above.

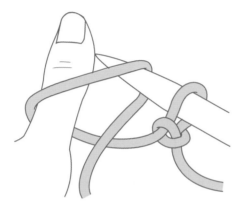

1. Loop around thumb

Hold the needle and the yarn from the ball in your right hand. Using the free end, make a loop around your left thumb, tensioning the yarn between your third and fourth fingers, as shown above. Insert the right needle tip.

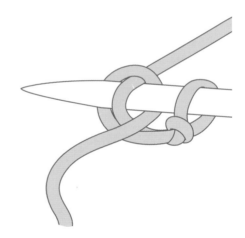

3. Through and off

Draw yarn through to make a stitch on the needle, as shown above. Release the loop from the left thumb, and gently pull the long end to tension the stitch.

LEFT-HANDED METHOD

This is suitable for those who hold the working yarn in the left hand: Loop the free end over the thumb, as above, but loop the ball end over the middle finger of the left hand; hold both yarn ends loosely with remaining fingers. Insert the needle under the thumb loop, then over the ball yarn and pull that yarn through.

LOOPING ON

The simplest way to cast on is to make a loop, as in step 1 opposite, then slip this loop onto the right needle. This method is generally used when you need to cast on extra stitches while knitting. Giving the loop an extra twist before placing it on the needle creates a firmer edge.

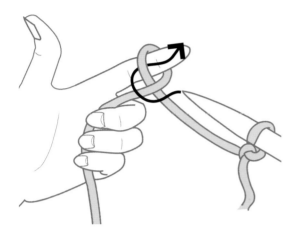

1.Twisting the loop

Loop yarn around the left thumb, insert the first finger down into loop and slip the loop off the thumb, twisting it, as shown above. Insert the right needle into the loop from left to right, as shown below, to create the stitch.

2. Completing the stitch

Release the loop from the finger, and pull end to close the stitch on the needle.

BINDING OFF

Lifting 1 stitch over the next secures the stitches and makes a neat edge for the knitting. Working every stitch as a knit stitch will give a chain effect on the edge; binding off in pattern will give a softer edge.

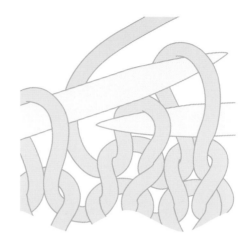

1. Lift over

Work the first 2 stitches. Use the point of the left needle to lift the first stitch over the second stitch and off the needle, as shown above. Work the next stitch, so there are 2 stitches on the right needle. Lift 1 stitch over and off the right needle. Continue until there is 1 stitch left on the right needle.

2. Fasten off

Break the yarn, draw the end through, and pull it tight to secure the last stitch.

MAKING A KNIT STITCH

Start by holding the needle with cast-on stitches in the left hand and the
empty needle in the right hand. The yarn from the ball hangs at the back
and, as described here, is also held in the right hand. Use your index finger
to loop it around the needle. If you hold the yarn in your left hand, tension it
by raising your middle finger and catch it around the needle in the same
way. Work into each stitch on the left needle in turn to complete a knit row.

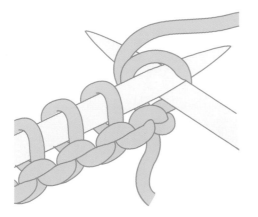

1. Winding the yarn in and around

Bring the right needle forward and under the left
needle; insert it from right to left (as shown above—
also called "knitwise") into front of first stitch; swing
yarn to the left, then up and around the right needle.

3. Pulling the stitch off the needle

Drop the stitch off the left needle to make a new stitch
on the right needle.

2. Pulling the stitch through

With the tip of the right needle, draw a loop of yarn
through the stitch on the left needle, as shown above.

HELP

**I really want to use a substitute yarn. What's the best
way to find a match?**

Check the information under "About This Yarn" given with
each project. Look for a yarn that's the same thickness and
texture. Be aware that if the fiber content is different, the
amount of yards/meters in your chosen yarn may not be the
same as the original, so you may need more or less yarn.
Finally, buy just one ball and check that you can match the
gauge given in the instructions and that you are happy with
the effect before purchasing a large amount of yarn.

MAKING A PURL STITCH

Hold the needles as you would for making a knit stitch, but bring the yarn from the ball to the front of the work. Work into each stitch on the left needle in turn, as described below, to complete a purl row.

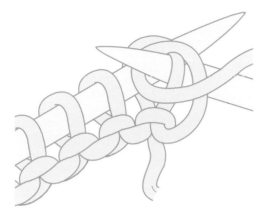

1. Winding the yarn in and around
Taking the right needle behind and under the left needle, insert it from right to left (called "purlwise") into the front of the first stitch; take yarn over and around the right needle.

2. Pulling the stitch through
Dip the tip of the right needle, taking it away from you to draw a loop of yarn through the stitch on the left needle.

3. Pulling the stitch off
Drop stitch off the left needle to make a new purl stitch on the right needle.

LEFT-HANDED METHOD

If you hold the yarn in the left hand, make sure to take the yarn over the needle before pulling it through; wrapping under the needle may seem easier, but your stitches will face the wrong way.

HELP

My knitting is uneven. What can I do?
If you have made a loose stitch, use the tip of a blunt-tipped needle to ease the extra yarn along the row to the side, where it can be woven or worked into the seam.

SIMPLE STITCH PATTERNS

Knit and purl stitches can be arranged to make many attractive stitch patterns.

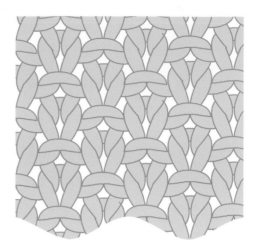

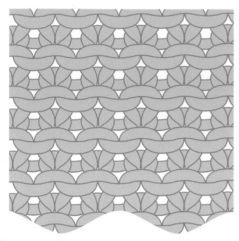

Garter stitch

Working over any number of stitches, knit every stitch of every row. The resulting fabric has alternate ridged and smooth rows on each side. To work purl garter stitch, purl every row.

Seed stitch

This is also called moss stitch. On an odd number of stitches, work alternate knit and purl stitches to the last stitch, then knit the last stitch. Repeat this row to make a textured, reversible fabric with alternating smooth and ridged stitches.

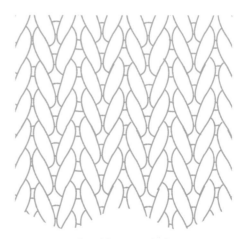

Stockinette stitch

Stockinette stitch

Working over any number of stitches, knit and purl alternate rows. All the smooth stitches are on one side of the fabric, while all the ridges are on the other side. The smooth side is stockinette stitch; the ridged side is called reverse stockinette stitch. In the UK only, this stitch is also called stocking stitch.

Ribbing

On an odd number of stitches, alternate knit and purl to the last stitch, and knit the last stitch. On the next row, alternate purl and knit to the last stitch, and purl the last stitch. The smooth and ridged stitches line up to make a reversible elastic fabric.

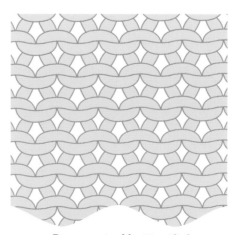

Reverse stockinette stitch

HOW TO CABLE

Cable-stitch patterns are made by using an extra, short double-pointed cable needle—to work the stitches in a different order along a row. All you need to know for the simple cables used in this book is how to cross three stitches over three on a knit row. For c6b, the stitches on the cable needle are held at the back of the work, and the cable slants to the right. For c6f, the stitches on the cable needle are held at the front of the work, and the cable slants to the left. The diagrams show a cranked cable needle—that's one with a kink in the center—because this kind of cable needle holds stitches more efficiently. However, you can use any short, straight needle or even, for large stitches, improvise with a blunt pencil or a wooden dowel with smoothed-off ends.

1. START C6B
Slip the first 3 stitches onto a cable needle and hold at the back of the work.

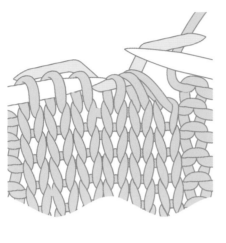

1. START C6F
Slip the first 3 stitches onto a cable needle and hold at the front of the work.

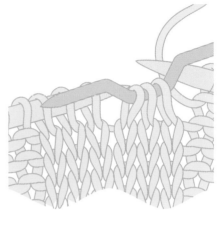

2. CONTINUE C6B
Knit the next 3 stitches.

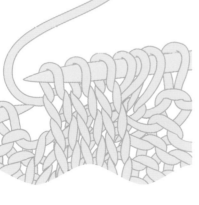

2. CONTINUE C6F
Knit the next 3 stitches.

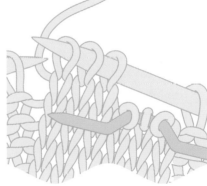

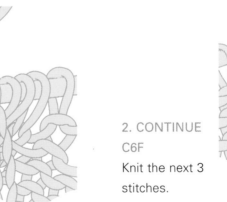

3. COMPLETE C6B
Knit the 3 stitches from the cable needle.

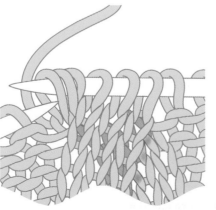

3. COMPLETE C6F
Knit the 3 stitches from the cable needle.

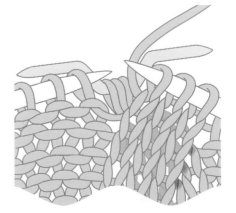

D16 (E0367- Knitting in no Time-
Correction On 1600)175#
Epson:01 _ PW-5 4th \ **Printting to C&C**

SHAPING AND PATTERNING

Increases and decreases can be used to shape pieces of knitting to make a garment or combined to create stitch patterns.

INCREASING

Each of these methods of increasing gives a different effect. The first makes a little bar at the base of the new stitch, the second is almost invisible, and the third makes a decorative hole.

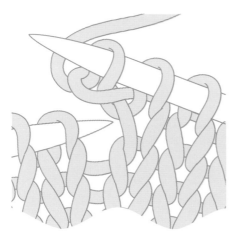

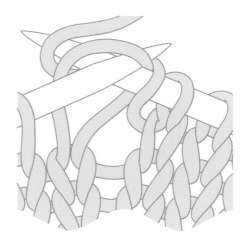

Knit into the front and back

Knit a stitch in the usual way, but do not drop the stitch off the left needle; take the right needle tip behind the left needle to knit into the back of the same stitch, then drop stitch off the left needle and onto the right, as shown above.

Yarn over

Between 2 knit stitches, bring the yarn between the needles to the front of the work and over the needle, ready to knit the next stitch, as shown above. Between a knit and a purl stitch, bring the yarn to the front, over the needle, and back to the front again. Between a purl and a purl, take it over the needle and to the front again. Between a purl and a knit, take it over and to the back.

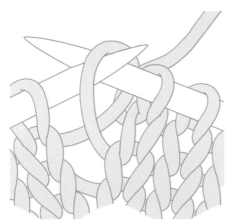

Lifted strand

Bring the left needle forward and, inserting tip from front to back of work, lift the horizontal strand lying between the needles. Take the right needle behind to knit into back of the strand, as shown above.

HELP

I can't afford to buy complete sets of every type of knitting needles. Which ones should I buy first?

Obviously, you'll need to start with the size needles given in the instructions, with maybe one size larger and one size smaller. Consider always buying medium-length (24 in./61 cm) circular needles because they are so versatile. You can use them to knit in rows for both small and large projects or in rounds for neckbands and whole garments. They are ideal for knitting projects on the go because you don't have to worry about prodding the person sitting next to you with the end of the needle. They also make good stitch holders!

DECREASING

To shape a garment, the first two methods, which are for decreasing one stitch, should always be worked in pairs, so that the fabric doesn't slant to one side or the other. The first two-stitch decrease is used mostly for lacy stitch patterns; the second two-stitch decrease can be used for both shaping and stitch patterns.

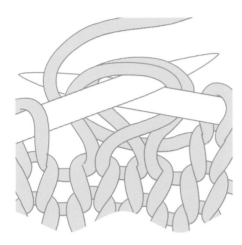

Knit 2 together

Insert the right needle knitwise through the fronts of the first 2 stitches on the left needle, knit them together, then slip both stitches off the left needle. The second stitch lies on top, and the decrease slants to the right.

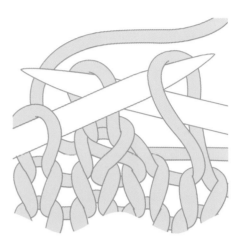

Slip 1, knit 2 together, pass slipped stitch over

Slip the first stitch knitwise, knit the next 2 stitches together, then lift the slipped stitch over and off the right needle. The slipped stitch lies on top and slants to the left; the knitted stitches underneath slant to the right.

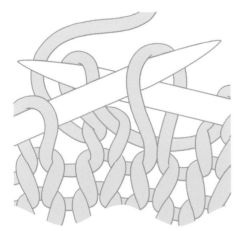

Slip 1, knit 1, pass slipped stitch over

Slip the first stitch knitwise, knit the next stitch, then use the tip of the left needle to lift the slipped stitch over and off the right needle. The first stitch lies on top, and the decrease slants toward the left.

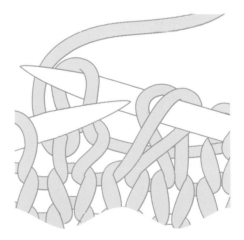

Slip 2, knit 1, pass slipped stitches over

Insert right needle through the fronts of the first 2 stitches on left needle as if to knit two together, but slip these stitches onto the right needle; knit the next stitch, then use the tip of the left needle to lift the 2 slipped stitches over and off the right needle. The center stitch lies on top.

MAKING GARMENTS

As your skills grow and you gain confidence, you'll want to try knitting something more ambitious. Creating hand knits gives you the choice of style and color, so your garments will always be unique.

UNDERSTANDING THE INSTRUCTIONS

Many of the knits in this book are very simple; but when you've chosen a project, read through the instructions before you start so you'll be sure you can cope with all the techniques needed. Here's a quick rundown of the things to look for.

Sizes

There's no need to consider sizes for wraps, scarves, and other accessories, but most garments are offered in a range of sizes. The smallest size is given first, followed by the other sizes in square brackets, separated by colons. Where only one figure is given, it applies to all of the sizes. The amount of room for movement, or ease, allowed depends on the fit of the design. Some of the garments are intended to be close fitting; others are generously sized. To find the size that's right for you, check for your bust size in the "To fit" measurements, then look at the corresponding figures given for the actual measurements of the garment. If in doubt about which size to make, compare the measurements with those of an existing garment that you already own and like. If you want a tighter or looser fit, simply follow the instructions for a smaller or larger size.

You will need

Some of the projects call for leftover or even improvised yarn, but where a certain brand is specified, please use it! All the designs have been created with the particular qualities of the chosen yarn in mind. If you use a different yarn, you won't get the same effect. You can sometimes substitute one yarn for another, but before you do, always make sure that you can achieve the same gauge with it (see below).

Gauge

The gauge of a piece of knitting is the number of stitches and rows produced over a given measurement. In order for the knitted item to be the correct size, the knitter must achieve the same gauge as the designer of the

project did. The recommended needle size is the size that was used to make the original item, and most knitters will get the gauge given using this size. Please, please, check your gauge! Start with the recommended needle size and knit a swatch, casting on slightly more stitches and working a few more rows than the gauge indicated, since the edge stitches will curl or distort.

Count and mark off the correct number of stitches and rows, avoiding the edges. If your marked stitches and rows measure less than they should, your knitting is too tight and the garment will be too small, so try again, using larger needles. If they measure more, your knitting is too loose and the garment will be too big; try again, using smaller needles.

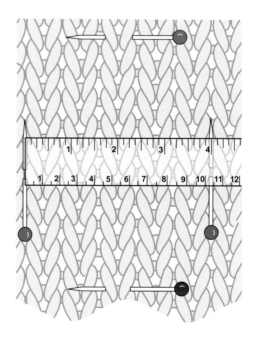

Measuring stitches and rows

Count off the number of stitches and rows given as the specified gauge and mark these off with pins, then measure between the pins in both directions.

Abbreviations

All the abbreviations you need to know for each item are given at the beginning of the instructions. Most abbreviations are very easy to remember, such as k for "knit" and p for "purl." Others look more complex but make sense once you realize that they actually explain a series of actions, such as sk2po for "slip 1 stitch, knit 2 stitches together, pass the slipped stitch over." Square brackets are used to show how many times a series of stitches or actions should be worked. Asterisks indicate where to repeat instructions or which part of the instructions to work again.

FINISHING

The edges of a garment are often finished by working into the edge stitches—either knitting or purling—and continuing the work on the picked-up stitches. The needle can be inserted into stitches or row ends, and the edge worked into can be straight or curved. For a neat finish, the trick is to place the needle consistently either into or between stitches along a row or 1 stitch in from the edge along row ends.

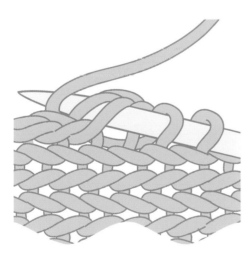

Picking up stitches from row ends

Join the yarn and insert the needle 1 stitch in from the edge, take the yarn around the needle, and pull a loop through to make a stitch. If you need to pick up fewer stitches than there are row ends, mark the edge into quarters, divide the number of stitches to be picked up into four, and pick up the same number from each section so you can be sure your stitches are spaced evenly.

SEWING SEAMS

The best way to sew seams in knitting is to work with the right side of the knitted pieces facing, so you can match stitches or row ends to create an almost invisible join. Using the tail of yarn left over from casting on or binding off makes a neat start. To join a new length of yarn, simply run the needle through a few edge stitches to secure the end, then bring the needle up to continue stitching. When the sewing is complete, weave in the yarn ends along the seams.

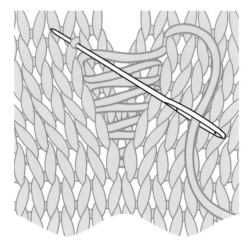

Mattress stitch

Use this stitch to join side and sleeve seams. Working from side to side alternately, insert the needle under the strand between stitches, 1 stitch in from the edge. Every 2 or 3 stitches, tension the yarn to bring the edges together.

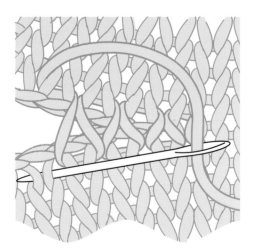

Mock grafting

This is a good way to match stitches when joining bound-off edges. Bring the needle up through the center of the first stitch of one side, then take it under both strands of the corresponding stitch on the other side and back down through the center of the first stitch. Bring the needle up

in the center of the next stitch, as shown below left, and continue joining stitches, tensioning the yarn every now and then to bring the edges together.

GRAFTING STITCHES

This is a way of joining stitches by working an imitation knit row, using a long end of yarn and a blunt-tipped needle. When stitches knitted in the same direction are joined, this join in stockinette stitch is perfect. If the two sections are worked in opposite directions, such as when joining a shoulder, the join will be a half stitch out but will still be almost invisible. Because the stitches have not been bound off, the join is soft and flexible.

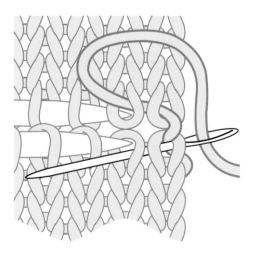

With the right sides of the knitting facing up, arrange the stitches to be joined on two needles with points to the right and with one set of stitches above and one below. Thread a blunt-tipped needle with a long end of yarn left over from the lower piece. Insert the needle up through the first lower stitch, down through the first upper stitch, up through the second upper stitch and down through the first lower stitch, then slip the joined stitches off the needles. Repeat to join all the stitches, as shown above.

MAKING A TWISTED CORD

Twisting strands of yarn together makes it stronger. The thickness of the cord will depend on the type of yarn and the number of strands used. The diagrams below show how to make a two-color cord; if you want just a one-color cord, place the knot at one end. Always allow plenty of yarn: The loop of yarn before twisting should be at least four times the length of the finished cord.

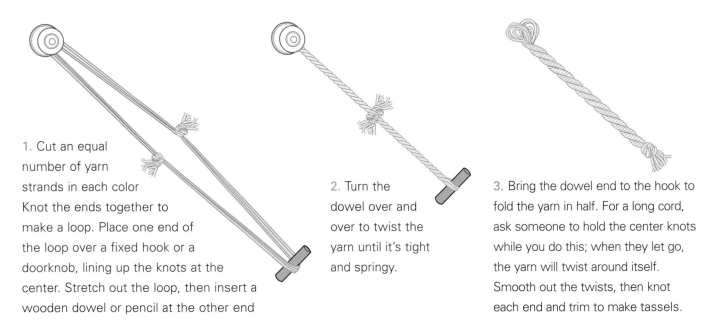

1. Cut an equal number of yarn strands in each color Knot the ends together to make a loop. Place one end of the loop over a fixed hook or a doorknob, lining up the knots at the center. Stretch out the loop, then insert a wooden dowel or pencil at the other end

2. Turn the dowel over and over to twist the yarn until it's tight and springy.

3. Bring the dowel end to the hook to fold the yarn in half. For a long cord, ask someone to hold the center knots while you do this; when they let go, the yarn will twist around itself. Smooth out the twists, then knot each end and trim to make tassels.

PICKING UP A DROPPED STITCH

Dropping a stitch is a beginner's nightmare. But don't panic. Pop the dropped stitch onto a stitch holder, then slip your stitches back to the place where you dropped the stitch. If the stitch dropped is only one or two rows down, you can pick it up with the tips of your needles. If it's dropped down farther, you'll need a crochet hook. Always check that a picked-up stitch is facing the same way as the other stitches before continuing to knit.

Picking up a dropped stitch with the needles

Insert the right needle into a dropped stitch, then stick it under the strand between neighboring stitches on the row above. Use the left needle to lift the dropped stitch over the strand and off the right needle. Slip stitch to turn it to face the right way, then slip stitches back to the correct place in the row.

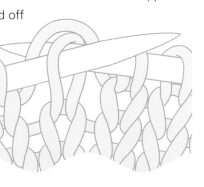

Picking up a run with a crochet hook

Insert a crochet hook into a dropped stitch, then catch the strand lying between the stitches on the next row up and pull it through to make a new stitch on the crochet hook. Continue until all strands have been turned back into stitches, then pop the last stitch onto the left needle.

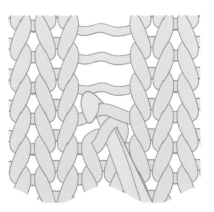

TEN TIPS FOR FASTER KNITTING

Of course, speed isn't everything; enjoyment, relaxation, and creativity come high on the list too! But there's no doubt that the faster you finish things, the more fun it is to go on to the next project.

1 Are you sitting comfortably? If you're too comfortable, squashed down into the sofa with your knees higher than your bottom, you won't be in a good position for knitting. Sitting upright, with enough elbow room to wield the needles, will get you knitting comfortably.

2 Do you have the right needles? Short needles, long needles, circular needles; wood, plastic, or aluminum. Some people love the bendiness of bamboo; others find that the stitches spring more quickly along rigid needles. Try using different types of needles until you find what works best for you.

3 Some of the world's fastest knitters use long needles and tuck the right needle under the arm, so that the right hand is free to move the yarn around the needle. Try it and see if it speeds up your knitting.

4 Knitting in the round can be quicker because you don't waste time turning the work and because the finishing is minimal.

5 New needles can slow you down. Give them a lick of furniture polish and a good rub with a soft cloth to break them in.

6 The nylon filament joining the tips of a circular needle can be irritatingly curly and springy. Smooth it out by dropping it into hot water, then pulling it through a dry cloth.

7 Try out different yarns. You might assume that the thicker the yarn, the quicker it will be to finish your knitting. While in some ways this is true because the stitches are big, actually making the stitches is slower. You'll pick up speed and form the stitches more quickly with a medium-weight, springy wool or wool-mix yarn.

8 Always start the yarn from the center of the ball. You might have to fish for this end, but once the yarn is flowing freely, you don't feel the weight of the ball of yarn, so your knitting will speed up.

9 Keep practicing until those first jerky movements flow together. Once you're on "auto-knit," the work will just grow and grow!

10 Finally, your knitting skills will never improve if you leave your work in a bag behind the sofa. Carry it with you! Don't be shy—knit everywhere!

RESOURCES

If substituting a yarn, please use the information given in the "About This Yarn" section for each project to find the nearest match.

YARN SUPPLIERS

IN THE UNITED STATES
COATS AND PATONS
Coats and Clark
P.O. Box 12229
Greenville, SC 29612–0229
tel: 800 648 1479
website: www.coatsandclark.com

ELLE
Unicorn Books and Crafts, Inc.
1138 Ross Street
Petaluma, CA 94954
tel: 707 762 3362
e-mail: dcodling@unicornbooks.com

ROWAN AND JAEGER
Rowan USA
4 Townsend West
Suite 8
Nashua, NH 03064
tel: 603 886 5041/5043
e-mail: rowan@westministerfibers.com

SIRDAR, DEBBIE BLISS AND NORO
Knitting Fever, Inc.
315 Bayview Avenue
Amityville, NY 11701
tel: 516 546 3600
website: www.knittingfever.com

IN CANADA
VILLAGE CRAFTS
1936 Como Lake Avenue
Coquitlam, BC V3J 3R3
tel: 604 931 6533
website: www.woolworks.org/stores/bc.html

ROMNI WOOLS
658 Queen Street West
Toronto, ON M6J 1E5
tel: 416 703 0202
website: www.romniwools.com

FLEECE ARTIST
1174 Mineville Road
Dartmouth, NS B2Z 1K8
tel: 902 462 0602

BIRCH HILL YARNS
#417 Avenida Place
12445 Lake Fraser Drive SE
Calgary, AB T2J 7A4
tel: 403 271 4042

RAM WOOLS
1266 Fife Street
Winnipeg, MB R2X 2N6
web enquiries: webmaster@ramwools.com

IN AUSTRALIA
COTTONFIELDS CRAFTS & YARNS
263 Stirling Highway
Claremont, WA 6010
tel: 08 9383 4410
website: www.cottonfields.net.au

SUNSPUN
185 Canterbury Road
Canterbury, VIC 3126
tel: 03 9830 1609
website: www.sunspun.com.au

THE KNITTING YARN SHOP
13 Lincoln Street
Laverton North, VIC 3026
tel: 03 9369 5944
website: www.knittingyarnshop.com.au

IN NEW ZEALAND

KNIT WORLD

PO Box 30 645

Lower Hutt

tel: 04 586 4530

website: www.knitting.co.nz

IN THE UNITED KINGDOM

COATS AND PATONS

Coats Crafts UK

P.O. Box 22

Lingfield House

McMullen Road

Darlington DL1 1YQ

tel: 01325 394394

website: www.coatscrafts.co.uk

DEBBIE BLISS AND NORO

Designer Yarns

Units 8–10

Newbridge Industrial Estate

Pitt Street

Keighley West Yorkshire BD21 4PQ

tel: 01535 664222

website: www.designeryarns.uk.com

ELLE

Quadra UK Ltd

Tey Grove

Elm Lane

Feering

Essex CO5 9ES

tel: 01376 573802

e-mail: quadrauk@aol.com

ROWAN AND JAEGER

Rowan Yarns

Green Lane Mill

Holmfirth

West Yorkshire HD9 2DX

tel: 01484 681881

website: www.knitrowan.com

SIRDAR

Sirdar Spinning Ltd

Flanshaw Lane

Alverthorpe

Wakefield

West Yorkshire WF2 9ND

tel: 01924 371501

www.sirdar.co.uk

INDEX

A
abbreviations, in patterns 153

B
bags
  black velvet 138–9
  cell-phone 134–5
  chunky-knit tote 116–17
  denim 114–15
  gold sequin 122–3
  knitting 128–9
  moss-stitch 124–5
  scrap mini-bag 140–1
  string 126–7
  tweed 136–7
  weekend 118–21
  woven-look 130–3
beaded cell-phone pouch 134–5
beaded-rib scarf 14–15
beads, threading 15, 135
binding off 26, 145
black velvet bag 138–9
blanket jacket 108–11
braid scarf 38–9
braids 20, 38

C
cable stitch 149
casting on 144–5
chevron poncho 70–1
chunky-knit tote bag 116–17
circular sweater 104–7
comfort wrap 56–7

D
decreasing 151
denim bag 114–15
diagonal scarf 12–13
dip-and-rip vest 96–9
dropped stitches, picking up 155

E
earflap hat 20–1
Fair Isle 28–31

F
Fair Isle earflap hat 28–31
Fair Isle fingerless gloves 32–3
finishing techniques 153, 154
fizz wrap 54–5
floppy-brim hat 34–5
fluffy shrug 62–5
fun-fur vest 82–5

G
garments, making 152–3, 154
garter stitch 148
gauge 152
gloves
fingerless 32–3
hand warmers 22–5
gold sequin bag 122–3
grafting stitches 154

H
hand warmers 22–5
hats
  earflap 20–1, 28–31
  floppy-brim 34–5
  pull-on 22–5

I
increasing 150
interlacing (*entrelac*) 131, 133

J
jackets
blanket 108–11
looped-edge 74–7
shaded 100–3
wrap 86–9

K
knit stitch 146
knitting bag 128–9

L
lacy scarf 10–11
leg warmers 44–5
leopard-spotted headband 46–7
loop-edged jacket 74–7

M
mattress stitch 154
measuring stitches and rows 152
mock grafting 154
moss-stitch bag 124–5

N
needles 150
circular 67
five (double-pointed) 22, 25
four (double-pointed) 22
holding 143

P
patterns, stitch 148
picking up stitches 153
pom-pom scarf 40–1
poncho, chevron 70–1
pull-on hat 22–5
purl stitch 147

R
rainbow scarf 36–7
reverse stockinette stitch 148
rib stitch 148
ribbed cowl, cream 52–3
ribbon-yarn wrap 58–9
ripped-fabric top 78–81

S

scarves
    beaded-rib 14–15
    braid 38–9
    diagonal 12–13
    lacy 10–11
    pom-pom 40–1
    rainbow 36–7
    scattered-sequin 42–3
    scrap-yarn 16–17
    skinny 26–7
    wavy 18–19
scattered-sequin scarf 42–3
scrap mini-bag 140–1
scrap-yarn scarf 16–17
seed stitch 148
sequins, using 122
sewing seams 154
shaded jacket 100–3
shaping 150–1
sheepskin-look vest 92–5
shrugs
    fluffy 62–5
    slouchy 66–7

skinny scarf 26–7
slip knot 143
slouchy shrug 66–7
sparkle vest 90–1
stitches 146–9
    dropped 155
    grafting 154
    measuring 152
    uneven 147
stockinette (stocking) stitch 148
string bag 126–7
striped afghan 60–1
summer shawl 68–9
sweater, circular 104–7

T

tassel wrap 50–1
techniques 142–55
tips 156
tweed handbag 136–7
twisted cord, making 133, 155

V

vests
    dip-and-rip 96–9
    fun-fur 82–5
    sheepskin-look 92–5
    sparkle 90–1

W

wavy scarf 18–19
weekend bag 118–21
woven-look bag 130–3
wrap jacket 86–9
wraps
    comfort 56–7
    fizz 54–5
    ribbon-yarn 58–9
    tassel 50–1

Y

yarns 7, 37, 152
holding 142
joining 12, 17, 18
stockists 157–8
two (for Fair Isle) 28

AUTHOR'S ACKNOWLEDGMENTS

Thank you to everyone who helped with this book; especially Debbie Bliss for mentioning my name! And to Cindy Richards for giving me the opportunity to work on this project; Georgina Harris for her enthusiasm and guidance; Tino Tedaldi for the lovely photographs; Sue Rowlands for the styling; Alison Shackleton for the design; Kate Simunek and Stephen Dew for the artwork; Kate Strutt for her modeling; and Sue Horan for her patience and thoroughness in checking the instructions.

For the inspirational yarns, thanks to Debbie Bliss and all at Designer Yarns; Mike Cole and all at Elle; Kate Buller and all at Rowan, Coats and Patons; and David Rawson and all at Sirdar.

Special thanks to Nancy O's and Valerie's in Ridgefield, CT, for coming to the rescue with props for the front cover photo.

For help with the knitting, thanks to Brenda Bostock; Sally Buss; Gwen Radford and Jean Trehane, and also to Gaye Bocock for realizing the Blanket Coat.

And finally a heartfelt "thank you" to Peter, who makes everything possible.